Thank you,
Enjoy the book
Jack

The Grand Tug of War
Buying and Selling in the Real World

Jack Willm

The Grand Tug of War
Buying and Selling in the Real World

JACK DILLON

LIGHTS ON PUBLISHING

The Grand Tug of War: Buying and Selling in the Real World
Copyright © 2022 Jack Dillon. All rights reserved.

Lights On Publishing
Tucson, Arizona

Jack Dillon
jackd@careerdividends.com

Cover & Typesetting by Valerie Willis
Edited by Erik Deckers
Images provided by ShutterStock.

All rights to the work within are reserved to the author and publisher. No part of this publication may be reproduced, stored in a retrieval system, or transmitted in any form or by any means, electronic, mechanical, photocopying, recording, scanning, or otherwise, except as permitted under Section 107 or 108 of the 1976 International Copyright Act, without prior written permission except in brief quotations embodied in critical articles and reviews. Please contact either the Publisher or Author to gain permission.

This book is meant as a reference guide. All characters, organizations, and events portrayed in this book are either products of the author's imagination or are used fictitiously. All brands, quotes, and cited work respectfully belong to the original rights holders and bear no affiliation to the authors or publisher.

Paperback ISBN-13: 978-1-7378208-2-6
Hardcover ISBN-13: 978-1-7378208-4-0
Ebook ISBN-13: 978-1-7378208-3-3

Table of Contents

Dedication VII
What's Inside This Book VIII
Foreword XI
In Memory XIII
Introduction 1
About The Author 5
Lessons to Grow Your Knowledge, Build Your Success . 8

From the Sales Desk 9

Section Titles 10
Lesson learned from Bill Sweet 13
Organization 14
Lesson Learned from Bill Heubach 21
Preparation 23
Lesson learned from Steve Brady 35
Planning 37
Lesson learned: Kevin McClellan 45
Communications 47
Lesson learned from Scott Smith 56
Execution 57
People 68
Leadership 71
Relationships 76
Selling Stew: Grand Lessons without the Theme 84
Attitude 95

v

SUCCESS.. 100
SUMMARY.. 106
ONE FINAL STORY 108

Thoughts at Halftime 110

From the Buyer's Chair 114

LESSONS TO GROW YOUR KNOWLEDGE, GROW YOUR SKILLS, BUILD
    YOUR CAREER 115
SECTION TITLES 116
LEADERSHIP 118
LESSON LEARNED: FROM THE AUTHOR 128
PREPARATION 130
PLANNING... 139
EXECUTION... 146
ORGANIZATION 155
MANAGEMENT 161
RELATIONSHIPS 169
COMMUNICATION..................................... 176
BUYERS' STEW 180
MARKETING 187
ATTITUDE... 189
SUCCESS.. 192
SUMMARY... 196

Million Dollar Takeaways............... 200

INTRODUCTION 201
MILLION DOLLAR TAKEAWAYS FROM THE BUYERS......... 257

In Conclusion 262

WHAT'S NEXT 263
ONE MORE THING 267
ACKNOWLEDGMENTS.................................. 270

Dedication

This book is dedicated to my wife Donna. For decades, she has forged the path for my success and happiness. Over the past three years, I have written two books, all while she provided the quiet to craft the words.

Donna is more than my wife, she is my friend, the person I cannot wait to find, to tell about my every win. As people age, they gain an appreciation for those things that slipped through the cracks during earlier days. There is no doubt, my appreciation for my wife has come full circle. She is the most honest, trustworthy person I have ever known. Donna is the reason for this book, and for the well-contented person staring at the screen at this moment. Thank you Donna for taking this trip through life with me. I'd do it all again. My love always.

What's Inside This Book

"The customer may not always be right ... but they are never wrong."

John Menichini, sales executive

This is not a book developed by only one person. This is a book constructed by dozens of very hard-working people, over decades, investing in thousands of meetings, exchanging millions of dollars. These people are stars not only because of their successes but because they developed the courage and the grit to get past *no*, regardless of how many times that word ended a presentation. This book includes:

Information to help a buyer learn new lessons and ideas from the inside, improve their overall business, add skills, grow their career, and think differently

Details for sales professionals, helping to better connect the dots to their buyers, building their business. It provides sales professionals the inside story of what buyers want, of how buyers think.

Amazing detail from dozens of interviews with buyers, sales professionals, and sales executives, opening the vault to decades of successful solutions built over many decades.

It provides specific ideas with great possibilities.

Although you will read stories from the past, the stories inside are about successful results, driven over time and through rejection, persistence, and extraordinary patience. We read history to learn. We read biographies of people we admire to learn from both their failure and success. This book, driven with stories resulting from past successes, will help you extract the critical nuggets, in order to help you assimilate superior ideas into your day to day efforts. When you uncover stories of successful people, executing within a similar world, you inevitably gain the skills and the confidence to better approach your world today, win the battle tomorrow.

When it comes down to the valuable success stories of working

with people, this book can be core learning for a new education, a new success plan for the road ahead. Lessons are everywhere. The specific lessons about success in buying and selling, of working with people, are inside these pages. Read both sides, no matter your role. As a seller, you want to know how your buyer thinks. As a buyer, you absolutely want to know what the offense has planned as they enter the field. There are success lessons inside. Now is the time to grow, to learn how to win in the real world.

Thank you,
Jack Dillon

Foreword

"What you do has far greater impact than what you say."

Stephen Covey

I was excited to hear Jack was writing a new book and that he was going to share some of his knowledge from his 40-plus years in business. I am honored to have known Jack for over 30 of those years. In all the time I have known Jack, he has always shown a great passion for his work and a great desire to strive for excellence. I have seen him mentor many co-workers and then stay in contact with them years after working with them.

I think one of the most telling things about Jack is how many of those former co-workers reach out to him when they need advice or counseling. He always taught me to make my circle of friends and contacts big. The more people you know, the more learning opportunities you possess. That has turned out to be some of the best advice I ever received. When working with him, I also learned the importance of being punctual and being prepared. Jack has become one of my most loyal friends and someone I highly respect for his professionalism. I highly recommend this read.

Bill Heubach

In Memory

Throughout our lives there are hundreds, maybe thousands of people who enter, sometimes for years, others only for a brief window. Many are quickly forgotten as they enter and exit without much fanfare. Others stay for a while, leaving a deep impression, they become unforgettable. They, in fact, leave such a hole, they become irreplaceable. This page is dedicated to two people who, as professionals, became a lasting part of my life and memory: Don Shin and Will Luckey.

Don Shin: Don was a young executive who started a new business in 2012. Over time, through determination, hard work, a unique set of products, and lots of luck, he created a successful organization which made great inroads in the sporting goods arena. I joined his team in 2014. Don was a professional on the rise. He surrounded himself with experienced people, all committed to helping him reach his goal. He was a good man, full of energy, huge dreams and charisma, lots of charisma. Over eight years, we worked together, striving to do things never done before. When everyone on the team had their doubts, there was Don, pushing and making sure we were "all in." He was young, energetic, excited for how he and his team were changing the future. Although I was there to help him, he taught me a great deal. He taught me about grit. That no matter how high the mountain, the job was to simply take the next step. He passed away early in 2022, far too young, far too soon. Because he had an oversized personality, he made many friends. He will be missed for a very long time. I was fortunate to see incredible achievements driven by a man who never thought any mountain was too high.

Will Luckey: In the largest role of my career, I got to work with key account managers and senior leaders of organizations. It's interesting how much we learn, when we hang around really smart, fascinating people. For many years I got to hang out with Will Luckey. He was my key account representative for the second-largest brand in our industry. He, however, was far more than just a key account rep, he was a smart man. He knew, in 2002, that the world was changing in a big way. To climb the ladder in a large organization, Will knew he needed to grow, learn and stretch far beyond his comfort zone. Working with Will meant more than just buying shoes and apparel. It was more about watching a sharp mind become sharper right before my eyes. He taught himself new technology, and then used it to increase business. Any time he was stymied by his organization, he did an "end around" and learned what he had to on his own. When there was no assistance, he did the work himself. Watching him taught me to move beyond my ego and away from the title on my business card. He taught me we all needed to learn a great deal more about the changing world. He was fun to be around. Although not young, he had a boyish look; I called him "Huck Finn." He helped my business, and he helped me. He too died far too soon. Will had a strong impact on my business, a larger one on my life. I miss Will very much. He made us all feel better about ourselves.

In life we get to meet lots of men and women along the journey. Maybe it's a good idea to step back, talk to them, learning what makes them tick. Maybe, just maybe, we can become better people in the process.

Introduction

"Education is not preparation for life; education is life itself."

John Dewey

This book was planned as a conversation with sales professionals from different industries. I wanted to write about things I experienced sitting with salespeople and their managers through the years. My aim was to stop many from posturing to sell me the kitchen sink and most of its fixtures.

I also wanted to teach new sales professionals how to successfully engage with experienced buyers, solving the issues of the day for each account. It was to be the instruction manual for sales professionals, written by a long-in-the-tooth, experienced buyer. This was to be a book to assist the sales pro to better understand what their buyer was thinking, feeling, and expecting during a presentation. After a few thousand words, the direction changed.

As I come to the end of my second book, I'm happy to say the thing that was to be a conversation has turned into more of a solutions-based book for both sides engaged in the *grand tug of war*.

The title says it all. This book is truly about a war, a systematic battle of real-life chess, played with real dollars. Certainly not a physical war, it's still a posturing on both the offensive and defensive sides of the desk. A battle where one side is pushing and maneuvering for a big order, while the other is on the defensive, looking to remain within budget.

The Grand Tug of War: Buying and Selling in the Real World

The buyer may be in need of product, but not as much as the sales pro is aching to sell. The buyer remains on guard, while the seller looks for the opening, the right phrase, or buying signal.

How does one write a book to include lessons and strategies from both sides of the desk? Once I recalled the efforts on each side, the ideas flowed. No matter where you sit, the advantage is to be educated on the information for each side: the buyer wants access to the seller's playbook, just as the sales pro wants to know every move the buyer will make.

In school, we all wanted the answers for every test. Having the right answers creates a better report card and rosier future. This book provides knowledge and direction, no matter which uniform you wear. It tells what to look for during a presentation, and can help you avoid some rather serious potholes, on either side.

Certainly much has changed since I began my journey. Technology has overwhelmed the process, no matter where you sit. There is one constant, however, that existed in 1979, and still does today: Relationships. The warm understanding between people makes this sport fun and worth playing. Getting into the scrum with smart, friendly people makes the paycheck feel almost like a bonus, like hanging out with industry friends becomes the reward. Over the decades, I've had the pleasure to learn from amazing men and women. Despite me being a cantankerous buyer, most people put up with me and my front-facing attitude. I've enjoyed many great relationships, and that's critical. No matter if you're a buyer or seller, spend a few extra minutes getting to know the people you joust with. Spend extra time enjoying the conversations and the experience. It's worth it; otherwise, it goes by all too fast.

This book offers lessons from real-life buying and selling that will save you time and stress, while providing practical ideas to maximize every presentation. This book can sharpen your view, enable you to see around corners, and protect your organization as you improve and expand your business.

It doesn't matter if you're a buyer or seller, the lessons can help you sharpen your execution. Offering two playbooks in one makes it easier for you to pick up signals and ideas the other side is planning for the battle ahead. Imagine if your favorite team had the opponents' game-day playbook every week! That is what you find inside: a playbook with executable ideas, no matter which side of the desk you own.

There are real lessons here, from everyday ups and downs, and the experience of thousands of battles. There is no theory or classroom learning enclosed. In addition to the lessons, there are the million-dollar takeaways — career life lessons from successful men and women that provide another level of detail to help you navigate today and the road ahead.

These takeaways, drawn from dozens of interviews, offer another facet to this masterclass. Gathering these grand lessons learned from successful men and women, became a great inspiration. Hearing about their trials, missteps, grit, determination, and persistence was a real joy. These Takeaways will provide not only great direction, but also personal motivation.

This book became a "twofer." The more I got into my experiences with sales pros, the more I realized the story would have been incomplete without chronicling both sides. It was important to provide the attitude from both sides of the presentation. Buying and selling is truly the greatest sport because it's how the world operates each and every day. Your favorite game, no matter how exciting, has a short season. Other sports begin and end, while the sales game never ends. It's the oxygen for the economy, the dollars that drive each day for all of us.

No matter which team you play for, information is currency. It provides power, confidence, and the critical detail to press forward, try new ideas, and avoid common mistakes. No matter how much you take from this book, spend more time enjoying what you do. Slow down, drink in the success you achieve, and the relationships you develop.

With this book, I leave it all on the field, as the sportscaster shouts after a grueling game. There is no additional information, no detail behind the curtain, no second volume. All of the necessary detail is located on these pages. Enjoy, learn, practice, and try again and again. I look forward to hearing from you. Because we each need to improve, I love feedback too, positive or not. Enjoy the read, enjoy your journey, and have a blast on the next playing field!

Jack Dillon
jackd@careerdividends.com
407-973-6136 | Orlando, Florida

About The Author

"The key to success is dedication to life-long learning."

Stephen Covey

Jack Dillon has been a part of the buying and selling community for fifty years. It actually began long before that first buying assignment in 1979. As a first grader, Jack was given the job of pretzel boy. During daily recess, he would go around the room to each desk, selling the five-cent pretzels. He continued to earn that role over and over for all eight years of his grade school career. Early on, he managed those nickel pretzels, selling out every day. Who knew that experience would lead to such a larger space in the buying and selling community?

Buying became a great love. Being able to buy for some of his industries' largest regional and national organizations was a joy on any day that ended in Y. Over time Jack grew into a good buyer with a reputation of being tough but fair. Although he never intended to have quite so many different stops along the journey, each new role brought more experience, combined with new skills. Just about every role was one he never wanted to give up. As new organizations grew, however, Jack saw the chance to build a bigger career through new opportunities. Each position brought him new relationships, greater wisdom and more and more success. It was a grand ride all the way until March 2010 when his role was eliminated, pushing him to the other side of the desk, the other side of the transaction.

In that world, Jack was able to take his buying skills and experience and support the many sales reps and accounts then part of his community. For more than twelve years, Jack had several leadership roles with organizations, helping each one build distribution and volume.

Along the way, Jack had the opportunity to learn from sales leaders who saw the world through very different eyes. It was all new, exciting, and rewarding. In the end Jack took his philosophy of "take care of the customer, no matter what" along with him to the other side. With his experience, Jack helped his teams add many new accounts over time. Although buying was his first love, selling and servicing accounts became an important new mission, as well as great joy.

Today Jack is a full-time consultant, speaker, and mentor to several managers throughout the United States. He is the lead blogger for golfincmagazine.com. In addition to his speaking roles, Jack enjoys writing about the new world of work, offering daily posts on Linkedin.

This is Jack's second book. His first: *Jump the Line: 101 Lessons for Professional Success* came out in September 2021. Jack enjoyed the everyday battles. He misses the energy of the *game*. He loved the scrum on each side of the desk, no matter which uniform he wore. He continues to look for new battles to win, and new opportunities. Reach out to Jack if you have a challenge where you'd like a fresh set of eyes. For special volume pricing on this book, contact Jack through his e-mail or phone. For consulting or speaking opportunities, please reach out in the same way.

For speaking engagements and book purchases in volume, please contact Jack directly.

Lessons to Grow Your Knowledge, Build Your Success

"Always put your customer first and it will come back tenfold. It is not what you sell your customer today that is important, but what you can sell them year after year."

Sam Aronson

"Treat every person the way you want to be treated. At the end of the day it didn't cost you an extra nickel to be nice."

William G. Baldwin Sr.

"Imperfect action beats perfect inaction every time."

Harry S Truman.

From the Sales Desk

Section Titles

- Organization
- Preparation
- Planning
- Communications
- Execution
- People
- Leadership
- Relationships
- Selling Stew
- Attitude
- Success

The grand tug of war is *the* greatest sport. Instead of just a three- or four-hour experience that takes place mostly in our living rooms, this amazing sport of buying and selling takes place every day, all day, throughout the entire business world.

It's nerve-racking, stressful, energizing, and life-fulfilling, making it our greatest sport. How could it not be when so many amazing men and women play, Monday through Friday, in every corner of the planet?

You can say whatever you want about relationships, this sport is about pure mental offense and defense. While the sales professional builds a story around great products, great service, and a trip together down the road of success, the buyer is on full alert, ready to put up their protective shield against the push play, the final effort to close the deal.

As the world moves faster, there is more at stake with every sales call. Sales professionals want to be on the e-commerce site, on the shelves, and deep throughout the warehouse. They will create what they believe is the strategy to make that happen. On the other side of the desk is the buyer, who comes into the meeting with a pile of data, detailing not only the story of this brand, but the numbers that indicate the overall health of the business. How much product might be purchased today? The data likely knows. In this new era of selling, it is information that will win games for either the seller or buyer.

Sales is a great way to earn a living. The opportunity to grow income comes down to how well the sales pro manages their day. Those who make that one extra sales call each day will eventually earn bigger rewards. Winning and losing can come down to any number of different factors: time, patience, attitude, follow-up, self-belief, openness, integrity, and trust. The buyer has to believe in the seller's sincerity and the truth of what is presented.

This is a sport of worry. The sales pro is always worried, consumed by the competitive brands that want to take more and more shelf space. They are concerned about relationships the buyer has with other sales professionals and what that might mean to business moving forward. The sales professional is constantly looking for more. They seem to always have their eye on the next potential conquest, winning more accounts, more orders, and consistently more replenishment.

It may sound like a tough way to spend a day or a decade, but professional sales is a wonderful profession. Just ask anyone who has built a great life around it. A sport, yes, the greatest sport! What game excites you every day? What sport can put unlimited dollars in your pocket? What sport can create a lifetime of friends in a wide community? In sales, every day is a game. A seller is working to sell, a buyer is open to it, but playing hard defense against what they cannot see. It is truly about coming equipped with a plan, a mission, and a specific list of goals. This is true for people on both sides of the desk. The buyer needs products, the seller has them. For the buyer, it comes down to setting boundaries and remaining within them, no matter the offer.

This section of the book — the Sales section — is broken down into 11 chapters with lessons from decades of buying, selling, and on-the-field observations. There are compelling stories to inform and teach. And lessons from successful men and women from different industries, people who have sold millions of dollars in products while earning millions in income.

Lesson learned from Bill Sweet

"I have been up against tough competition all my life. I wouldn't know how to get along without it."

Walt Disney

Bill has served the same territory for a long time. Buyers trust Bill. They give him time to present and the opportunity when the story feels right. He has earned his place in their business and their hearts. At the same time, Bill is tough. He has no problem going toe-to-toe with his suppliers to make certain his accounts are managed well. He can be a true thorn in the side of a problem. He works it until his customer wins. That is why Bill has remained a favorite with both his accounts and suppliers for decades. Here is one of his stories:

> "I received a call from a customer wanting to see me about ordering a specific product. When I arrived, he was ready to give me the quantity of the product order when I asked him to hold that order until I could show him the products for the rest of that category. I proceeded to present the product lineup and received an order. I then asked to go back to the original conversation about the product the customer wanted, and he decided he wanted to connect to other suppliers before he made a decision. (Lesson: take the easy order. Never put the customers' wants on hold.) PS: I never got the order."

Organization

Creating and maintaining structure in your workday is essential to succeeding in sales. Managing your calendar helps you get the most out of every day. Sales professionals love what they do because of the freedom it provides. Moving away from an office and hitting the road to serve accounts is appealing to many. However, it takes constant oversight to keep each day on track. Being organized will allow you to see more people and attract more sales. As you think about your work, think about time, account management, timely order placement, follow-up, and managing problems. They are all important and vital to your success. Building self-discipline into your work will create distinction in your plan and your execution.

PROFESSION FOR A LIFETIME

You made a smart and purposeful decision the day you began to sell. It may have involved a plan or maybe you needed to work. The reason doesn't matter. Just know this: the best sales professionals are some of the highest earners in all of business. Deciding to sell requires more than saying yes, acquiring a vehicle, organizing samples, and setting up appointments.

You'll quickly realize you need to work out a plan to finance the next three years of your life. This is more than true if you become an independent sales professional with no real safety net waiting below. It's critical to set up a budget for both your fixed household expenses and travel costs, especially in the first eighteen months. Sales success takes time. Even after you write orders you won't be paid the bulk of that income until the orders ship, or in some cases when the invoices are paid.

Doing the work each day, no matter the results, will pay dividends over time. Just know that success won't happen overnight. Establishing your likability and trust are the forerunners to writing big orders. In addition to building your personal story, it's important to build the value of your brand with your prospects. Taking over a territory means you have a group of clients already doing business with the brand. It is important not to reinvent the wheel but to build very solid, personal relationships. When people like you, they will invite you back, spend time, and hopefully buy from you in the short term. Earning time in front of the customer is the fastest path to building a business. Your efforts will result in building a successful territory: one you can manage for years and years. The beginning in any territory as a new rep is all about establishing trust and credibility. This foundation will allow you to grow. It will also be great for referrals, as buyers are always chatting about brands, products, and people.

The learning curve is longest at the start. Don't fret about your numbers out of the gate. Your goal should include seeing as many past customers as possible in the first 90 days. Showing up is 80% of the battle. As you get to know the important buyers, it is critical that these buyers get to know you, too. Although the focus will always be on your customer, buyers will be more comfortable working with you when they know you. Before you get in front of customers, be certain to practice the pitch about the brand and products. When you are in front of buyers, the focus is all on them. This includes listening to the buyer, staying on point, and meeting the objectives of the sales call. After every meeting, sending a thank you note will help build your story. Although it takes time to build success, sales is a grand profession.

Here are a few thoughts for the sales professional:
- Call your customers regularly, if only to say hello.
- Timely follow-up, done well, will earn recognition that will pay handsomely over time.

- When you have an upset customer, attack the issue with a sense of urgency.

- Thank customers for their time and business.

- Respect the customers' time by being early for appointments.

- If drop-ins to certain accounts are not welcome, stop dropping in.

- Give your customers good news fast and bad news faster.

- Always tell the truth. Buyers can handle the truth.

- Be humble and talk about them and their business. The "I" should remain on the other side of the door for client meetings.

- As a supplier, knowing where you fit and how best to provide value are critical stepping stones in building both relationships and success for the long term.

Keeping score

Whether you represent one organization or several suppliers, you are a team of one out in the field. Although you are probably receiving regular reports about your territory and accounts, that data is coming back to you from the supplier(s). Because your mission is also to capture client information beyond the numbers, it can be a valuable habit to keep a written journal of each business day. This journal can include meeting highlights, opportunities, account concerns, and other valuable information expressed during any buyer encounter. Building a book of account information is like owning the master playbook for every account. Take those daily observations and write up a weekly summary. As buyers change, you can always refer back to previous ideas that may prove valuable to the new buyer. A short record of each major sales call can be an asset that will pay dividends over the long term.

Keeping score, part 2

Just like watching sports, you know who's winning just by looking at the scoreboard. In sales, finding the score can be just as easy. Over morning coffee, pull up the updated company report. Review your monthly production, including the number of orders, total dollars written, and total dollars shipped. There are other benchmarks to understand, however. This is important to note, especially on days when new orders just don't seem to happen. When the day runs dry, there are other ways to build business. When you are not creating sales, build relationships with your customers. Gather intel about customers and competitors that can pay off down the line. Gather inventory information on customers, so you have an idea of when they may need to place a new order. Although the numbers will ultimately determine the success of the territory, there is no reason to sulk or slow down when buyers just aren't ready to buy. Understand that building the territory involves so much more than receiving a purchase order. Sitting in your office waiting for your buyers to call is never a winning strategy. Being face-to-face, reinforcing your care and concern for the buyer, providing ideas and information are essential steps in earning your stripes. Just as any professional league has a pre-season training period followed by practice games, you should prepare in a way that puts you in line to write orders in the future.

The home office

As a sales professional, you will spend a great deal of time on the road, traveling to your accounts, and working face-to-face most weeks of the year. The road is where it happens. Buyers want to see you, see the product, and know they'll be receiving great value for their investment.

The more business you write, the more office work you create. Your home office is a valuable piece of your program. Much more than a room with a laptop, your office is that space where you pull together all of the plans, hopes, and dreams of the buying season. I can't tell you how to build your office, because it depends on your industry and business. But it's to build a space where you can do all of your work in comfort and without interruption. It's also where you will now have virtual visitors. Thanks to technology, you'll be part of virtual calls in that space, so you want a clean, presentable space that tells people who you are.

From the hardware, lighting, books, and photos you show, your office is now open for business. In a world where virtual meetings take place daily, your office should always be ready for guests. Be proactive with the image you present. Your home office is an integral part of your operation. Treat it as such, always searching for the next tool or upgrade that will help you improve your home office space.

Record keeping

It's critical that you keep track of all your important records to monitor expenses, receive reimbursement, or file receipts for that ever-important tax date, April 15th. You may want to consult an accountant in order to set up a system that's easy to manage. Whether you are an independent or company sales professional, there are essential records to keep. Once you have the proper template built, be certain to update the records weekly. Falling behind is easy and problematic. It will make for long nights, lost weekends, and time away from driving new business. Take it from an all-pro procrastinator, stay current with all detail involving your organization, your expenses, and your income.

Cost of doing business

There is no book you can buy that will tell you the exact, yearly, out-of-pocket expenses you might incur in your role. As an independent, it can run $40,000 or higher, depending on your industry, size of your territory, and other specific factors. Before the recent fuel spikes, yearly travel costs in my industry ran well over $40,000 on average. With more buyers accepting virtual meetings as a way to talk with sales reps, there are ways to reduce costs. However, those calls will not work for new product presentation meetings, or when a large account has a problem.

Don't assume your buyers will accept a virtual meeting. Get

their feedback before you assume any shortcuts. Today, it simply costs more to work as a sales professional. It might be a good idea to reset the way you travel your territory, the route, number of overnights, and so on. If you're still working to understand the playbook, speak with your sales manager as well as a few older sales reps who have been through managing a territory. In the end, if you can do more business while traveling less, you'll end up putting more money in your pocket. It is a good idea to keep a travel journal. Once you write up daily notes on everyday expenses, you can build spreadsheets to keep records of the different expenses. As you build future plans, talk with your buyers and your manager, making sure the critical people of your community are in agreement.

TEAMWORK

The most valuable part of your sales efforts is face-to-face interaction with customers. Although you can have virtual meetings, a face-to-face meeting is still the best way to create a sale and a customer. There is much to do before you can close the sale. You have to fill your calendar with appointments, which might be the toughest part of the work. One suggestion: after the appointments are booked, confirm each one 24 – 48 hours beforehand.

Once you have written orders for the week, they must be properly handled and sent to your organization. Check each order for accuracy first.

A new, important part of selling is marketing, especially social media marketing. Work with your marketing department and even your accounts to create interesting posts about your products and story. Post testimonials from happy customers for more social media exposure.

Consider hiring a virtual assistant, a person with the special experience you require. They can live almost anywhere; you can pay them through your smartphone, and they can lighten your workload. When you have too many items that keep you away from customer contact, an assistant can manage your administrative labor. When there is much to do after the order, look at the many ways to build an inexpensive support system: one that takes the less valuable items off your calendar. After all, managing your time is the ultimate factor in the level of your success.

LOYALTY

Whether you represent one brand or several, loyalty should always be one of your foundational principles. Organizations like consistency; they want to keep sales professionals in place. They know that changing out a rep in any territory may lose accounts as well as 20% or more in sales volume. Today, however, loyalty is a value seemingly harder to find. On one hand, the sales rep is always looking to make more money. The organization is looking to develop larger accounts, grow sales, and sell more items per account. In corporate sales, organizations group territories as A, B, and C territories. They know they have several A territories, yet constantly wonder why more territories cannot produce "A" results.

The sales professional, on the other hand, is always looking to improve and find a better way to grow both accounts and revenue. Once a year, take the time to step back and do some research. What is changing in your industry? Who are the brands moving up and moving out? Who are the new customers, growing customers, and customers losing market share? What are the leading reps in your industry doing that is new, different, and effective? What new apps and software can make you more productive?

Because you are on the go constantly, with your head down, you can easily miss many changes happening all around you. This time out might give you some great new ideas, help you meet new people, and tweak your journey enough to make a real difference. Being comfortable with the same old routine is not a good thing. It's a dangerous way to operate. Know that brands get stale, products get old and sales reps fall into routines. So, at least once a year, become an observer rather than a doer. Dig into what is new and different. Stay out front by learning what is coming down the highway. Be excited by the changes. It pays to be at the front of the line.

Lesson Learned from Bill Heubach

"A passive approach to professional growth will leave you by the wayside."

Tom Peters

Bill is, first of all, a gentleman. He is not only a top executive within his organization, he also sells and manages accounts across the country. Bill believes in being upfront and honest while providing thorough follow-up. He goes all out to do what he can, sometimes realizing that it sometimes may not be enough. He gets up every morning with one goal: to take care of his customers. Bill is not only a wonderful teacher, he is a great mentor. Here is a classic story from the road.

> "I was flying back into my local airport after a long business trip, when I received a call from the boss, explaining he was having a serious problem with a key customer. Since I had to drive to the office to pick up additional samples for upcoming appointments later in the day, I went to find the boss before I left. I grabbed the samples and headed out. What I did not realize is that the boss opened up the back door of my van, adding even more samples. He did not, however, close the van door. As I was driving down the major highway near the office, I saw a car behind me working to dislodge a shirt from his windshield using his wipers! In addition, it turned out that someone recognized my van with shirts flying out of the back and decided to call the local radio show. The on-air DJ announced my company

was conducting a free shirt giveaway on the highway! I happened to be tuned into that station at that moment. All of a sudden the horns all around began to honk. I pulled over and shut my van door.... minus a few samples."

Preparation

Every meeting with a buyer is about dollars and cents. It is about service, quality, and value. The buyer has prepared for this meeting and done the necessary homework. Are you ready? What have you done to maximize your time and opportunity with the buyer? Preparation separates strong sales professionals from poor performers. Those who are confident and ready to present will certainly succeed over the long term. In sales, "winging it" rarely results in getting large purchase orders from any buyer. Coming in knowing the numbers and your competition, understanding as much as you can about the current opportunity, will help you build your business. Even if it takes three or four meetings to reach a conclusion, come ready to ask the right questions, answer tough questions, and build confidence.

What Buyers Want, Part One

In my first buying assignment, I was excited for the opportunity. I wanted to learn as quickly as possible. It was important for me to make solid buys each and every time. In order to do that, I was going it alone. I expected and wanted no help from the outside; I was a long way from trusting people beyond my organization. I prepped for every meeting, believing that homework was enough. Eventually, I learned who I could trust among the suppliers. Each buyer is different, unique in their own way. Even if there were a book on buying (like this one, perhaps?) buyers work for individual organizations. They develop their own style. As the salesperson, you have your own organization to deal with and your own style.

As you grow your territory, it's important to develop your own playbook. Each section should be titled by the name of the business and not the individual buyer. Buyers change, so you want to develop one nice, neat book of history and experiences with each account. As buyers change, you continue with the section and simply change out the buyer information. Buyers have a boss, just as you have a sales manager. They have sales goals, gross margin goals, inventory targets, as well as other benchmarks. Although the smart buyers will not be telling you the company secrets, you can move towards the inner circle by providing real opportunities to help the buyer build larger margins through special programs, as well as off-price opportunities. Spend time getting to know each buyer as a person, and then spend time learning how each operates their business. Buyers want to be treated as people.

WHAT BUYERS WANT, PART TWO

Sales professionals are fairly certain they know what their buyers want and need, but no one is a true expert. To help remedy the confusion, I have organized a want list developed by someone who served for decades as both a buyer and a seller. As you work your territory, you may want to test a few. As more and more ideas work for you, you might want to add a few more to the test:

- Buyers want products their organizations can sell.
- Buyers want the complete story on delivery timelines, shortages, and cancellations.
- Buyers want good news fast and bad news faster.
- Buyers do not want surprises.
- Buyers want the ad and social media plan from the start.
- Buyers never like products showing up, unannounced without approval.
- Buyers want fast, thorough follow-up.
- Buyers want you to work at least as hard as they do with

regard to your brand.

- Buyers want to know what you can do and will do in order to resolve problems.

- Buyers want frequent communications. Just check in.

- Buyers want to be thanked and recognized for their business.

- Buyers want a sense of urgency, responding to goods not selling.

- Buyers are happy to help you when there is an honest, open 2-way relationship.

- Buyers like simplicity.

- Buyers want you to do the heavy lifting.

- Buyers want to impress their boss.

- Buyers love to buy.

- Help your buyers win in their individual situations.

THE PITCH AND MORE

Over time the sale professional develops a presentation that gets to the important product and program points in a specific amount of time. As experience kicks in, the rep will speak less and listen more. When I was a young retail guy on the sales floor, I believed the more the customer learned about the product, the more sales would happen. So I talked and talked until eventually, I learned the opposite was true. Sales were getting complicated, not simpler with my non-stop information spillage.

The successful pitch involves lots of listening. The times you'll want to speak are with the questions you want to ask, the essential details you need to gather. Develop your critical questions that will enable you to move towards a yes. Besides the critical questions, the assets in a great pitch include talking about the prospect and their business, providing important details about your products and programs while listening intently, taking detailed notes. Think of your customers and prospects as friends, people you want to grow with over time. Careers are long. If you remain in the same territory, even if you change organizations, you can end up serving the same accounts for years. Today is the day to begin building relationships with every buyer with access to dollars to spend. Remember that friends buy from friends, so the better the relationship, the greater the opportunity.

THE PITCH, PART TWO

Know that every account is unique. Even when things appear to be the same out front, each one is unlike any other business you will work with over time. You will have a direction to take, one path with a flow, questions, and a plan to move all buyers to your side. But there is also the need to be ready to adjust as your buyer brings new information to every meeting. Will you be prepared?

There are no hard and fast steps to a final agreement. Pitfalls and detours can appear at any time during a presentation. Be prepared to move in new directions as you receive feedback from the buyer. Your most important step at any point is to listen, to say nothing, allowing the buyer to have the stage. There will be time for questions. Listening is a great tool and your most valuable asset in the moment.

Also, presenting is not memorization or showing buyers how smart you are. It's a gathering exercise. You are looking for all the detail you need to find out. In any product presentation, there will be nuggets of information the buyer shares that are critical to remember. Uncovering these nuggets is one goal of the pitch.

With much of your time spent listening while adjusting for potential curveballs, receiving straightforward, complete answers will allow you to move forward. Coaches in every sport adjust the plan during the game; adjusting in sales has the same high value. Be prepared to adjust based on new information you receive.

BE BEYOND PREPARED

Here are the three essentials for successful selling.

- Develop and use great listening skills.
- Be early, every time.
- Be beyond prepared for every account meeting, for each unique buyer.

That's it! All you need to know to build a lucrative career is right here. Do these three things well and you will earn money beyond your largest dreams. However, these three seemingly simple essentials miss one important problem: Life tends to get in the way on many days.

Let's focus on the third lesson: to be beyond prepared for every meeting. If you're about to meet with an existing account, you have a history. You can do a great deal of specific research. The buyer wants to know what is new and different. How can they bring more excitement and sales to the organization?

Setting up a great story for new products or programs gives you a chance to draw the buyer in. You can provide information about your brand, industry, or territory that this buyer will find useful. Bringing information to the buyer is important, as many are tied to their office much of the time. They are looking for information that can impact their decisions and business. As you provide new, valuable information, you become more of an insider, one who will be more welcome than the average sales professional. Your mission is to become much more than another rep in their contact list.

BEFORE THE SALES CALL

You need to prepare a strategy with a series of goals. You should also follow up with a meeting, complete with ideas and suggestions. Your buyer is busy, so it's up to you to provide this valuable information. Good buyers will always be prepared for important planning sessions or new product meetings, but they may not be very well prepared for several other check-ins throughout the season. If you're going to see a buyer, that meeting must have a purpose and an agenda, at least from your side. Otherwise, you're just wasting your buyer's time.

Being prepared means providing new information your buyer can use. There's an acronym that I use frequently: WIIFM, or "what's in it for me." Everyone you meet has this on their mind. They're thinking, what new, usable information can this person bring me? What can they do for me?

They're looking for purchasing data on their account, territory success with your products, and information that can support any investment in your brand. New information will open up new conversations, create orders, and even trials for new products. As you prepare for each meeting, think about the ten-year accumulated effect of solid preparation. The change in the numbers can be off the charts. Be totally ready on all fronts and look to always bring new, important information they can use. Never waste their time or take it for granted.

Ask Lots of Questions

After decades as a buyer, I switched to the sales side of the desk. Being in sales development was a great step because I came in with a unique point of view. Now, after years in sales, I still think about ways to improve. How can I get better at each phase of the process? By the time I joined the sales side, I had decades of experience.

Looking back, there were some important improvements I could have made. Two of them include: 1) Always assume the buyer knows your products and services; and, 2) Do not go into a meeting preaching about the greatness of your brand or product. Assume they have done some homework in preparation for the meeting. The more business they do with you, the more time they will likely spend preparing.

Another important change: Other than small talk, I would limit my conversation to asking questions that will enable you to move toward a sale that day. Any sales rep can get into trouble when they become the expert in the room.

If I were starting my sales career today, I would build a meeting plan to be about listening with focus to the buyer, answering the buyer's questions, and speaking only when asking questions that provide value. I would also be ready to adjust, be flexible, and never firm in my approach. It's vital to gain the confidence of the buyer. It's important for the buyer to feel comfortable.

Less time means a sharper focus

The buyer's world moves ever faster, in new and different directions. There are more obligations, more to-dos, and more responsibilities. That means less time for sales reps. It also means less focus with a full calendar. The time for sales appointments has been squeezed — the buyer wants you in and out quickly. How will you adjust? How can you achieve more in less time? We can all be sure that this will not change. You'll never have endless time to get your points across. This makes your preparation all the more valuable. A few ideas include:

- Break down all historical sales numbers with the account.
- Present pricing in a simple spreadsheet.
- Present programs or specials in bullet form. They're easy to read and comprehend.
- If you know the account, offer two or three order suggestions.

The more you are prepared to help, the more business can be written. Ending a sales call with "I'll have to think about it" is a very poor ending. It's critical to gain a positive decision or a simple "yes" to one of your suggestions. Buyers must make good decisions in less time. That's where your support comes in. Be ready to assist them in moving forward by keying in on the important details about the buyer and their business.

What your buyer knows

In my first full year as a buyer, the world relied on catalogs, sales reps, and peers to learn about products, better pricing, and the essential detail we needed before we spent a dime. Those days were slow, limiting, and frustrating.

Today is very different. Today's buyer learns a great deal about brands and products long before any appointment. They're looking everywhere for both good and not-so-good news about their suppliers. They're more diligent because they can do it in less time.

Although I just laid out the world of the buyer as it should be, never assume the buyer knows all your details as you skip the meat of the presentation. Provide the full story; the buyer will cut you off, telling you what they want to know when you provide unnecessary information. Never waste time with details unless they're important to the sale.

Some things you'll want to talk about include product availability, best pricing, and the marketing budget and schedule. Talk about how you and your organization will help support new product launches. Spend your time on those things the buyer does not know but should. The days of providing catalogs, of telling drawn out stories of features and benefits are done..

WHAT PROSPECTS NEED TO KNOW

Prospects, unlike customers, have yet to invest in you or your brand. They're interested, but they probably haven't spent much time gathering information. If you can turn several prospects each year into consistent accounts, you build long-term distribution. This is what every organization wants. And because prospects are not yet customers, you probably don't know a great deal of real information about them. Therefore, if you can gain time on a prospect's calendar, the first meeting is an exploration. Once you gather the details you need, your next meeting will be more about your brand, products, and what your organization can do to support and serve them.

After your first meeting, the prospect will probably take a deep dive into your products. They'll want to know who sells it locally and nationally. They'll dig into your e-commerce platform, and whether you protect the advertised retail pricing across the various channels.

One important goal in the first meeting is to be liked. If you come across as someone who is all about service and genuinely cares about the account and its success, you will have a solid chance to do business. Your focus is now on getting the account open. The size of the first order isn't that important. It will not be an indication of the future size of the business. It's your service and execution of the orders that will eventually determine the size of the account. If you're looking to gain trust, provide testimonials. Buyers hang out and talk with other buyers. Provide a list of other buyers and accounts who trust you and succeed in selling your products. If the buyer has doubts, suggest a small test of your better products. Create a program that you know will work. It is then important to support this test in any way you can.

Once the test goes well, you have earned a larger shot. Continue to be cautious, working with your top movers. No reason to have this new account take any risks at this time. When I was the buyer in this situation, I needed to be comfortable with the sales rep and the sell-through. I would ask myself, "Can I sell this product?" If the lights turned green, I looked for a better program and price. If I had doubts, I put things on hold. Buyers need to feel comfortable with both you and your process. Prospects are likely total rookies when it comes to your story. Prioritize the fact that you must be liked before you become this buyer's new friend.

BEYOND THE TARGETS

No doubt, you have several targets your sales manager has given you. You may have sales goals for the month, quarter, and year. Not to mention account goals, distribution goals, and even goals to reactivate inactive accounts. And you have no doubt created self-directed targets. These numbers are all important. Once you have reviewed and digested the goals, take a step back from the numbers to view the work beyond the spreadsheets.

Buyers have their own targets, concerns, and fears. As you plan each meeting, it's important to consider the buyer as an individual person as you build your presentation. Developing relationships is a critical skill as you grow your territory. Just know that any time you're working with people, the unexpected can and will happen. Although you have a series of targets to achieve, the buyer has their own program and plan for you and your product. It's important to bring both patience and empathy into the sales meeting. The ability to see the world from your buyer's point of view is the day you will see the opportunity with 360-degree vision.

The only way to achieve your targets is through people. No matter the size of your goals or vision of success, it's essential to get the people thing right, in order to create long-term relationships. Building and sustaining relationships is a critical part of your business. It's the path to long-term success. Maintain open and friendly communications with every account. Invest your time and energy into those people who can create and build your business. To reach those targets, you must create relationships that work for your buyers.

SECRETS

The following lessons are not secrets, but they have been pushed to the side by many experienced salespeople, often to their own detriment. The two secrets are:

- Be the most prepared person in the room.
- Be early for every appointment.

Preparation is the secret sauce for success. When you go into a meeting, you want to be confident, patient, and prepared for success. Preparation provides insight that's just not available without doing the work. It uncovers the necessary details and facts for any meeting. On any given day, you may be working to open a new account, reopen a lost account, or get a signature on a large sales order. No matter why you're there, be ready with the critical information. Winning the battle is not so hard when you are prepared. Work to become the smartest person in the room for that meeting. The sharpest people want to hang out with the person in the know.

BE DISTINCT OR EXTINCT

There are hundreds of thousands of salespeople throughout the United States selling all types of products and services. On most days, these men and women work to open new accounts, write larger orders, and build careers that have real staying power. Who are they? What traits make the great ones great, while the rest continue the search for their unique offering? What makes one person a star, the next a lost soul, barely able to pay the monthly bills? Understanding and learning the important skills of the day will help put a sales pro on the right track. With business moving ever faster, there will be new skills to acquire for tomorrow. As you keep up with this ever-changing information, you will also become sought out by other organizations.

Although there are unique skills needed in becoming a top-notch sales pro, there's no magic to it. It's about becoming consistent, creating and maintaining daily discipline, and doing timely follow-ups. It's also about understanding your organization and industry beyond your workplace. It's about understanding your customers, anticipating the needs of your top 20% of accounts — that's where 80% of your results may come from.

Being distinct does not mean being so different that customers will not recognize your efforts. When a salesperson executes the fundamentals day in and day out, they stand out. That's when they become distinct. The flip side is to do the bare minimum: barely show up, offering little or no service. To succeed over many years, do all you can for your buyers, then do a little more.

Always a Rookie

As I write this, the world is still in limbo, looking to shake off the effects of COVID-19. We're experiencing high inflation and supply chain issues. We all fell into the pandemic without any experience of how to handle it. We were rookies, looking to the government and each other for any path forward. We're almost out now and feeling mostly normal again. As organizations look to bring people back to the office conflict exists on both sides.

We are headed to an unknown future. Maybe not in business, as that seems to be getting back to normal. We know that leaders and organizations will continue to fight to lower costs and maximize profit wherever they can. Think driverless trucks, driverless taxis, and robots in the warehouse picking orders. At the same time, new jobs and entire new industries will be created due to ever-changing technologies.

Business is moving faster than ever. Yes, experience and skills will be real assets in navigating the world beyond today, but it may take even more trial and error to give us additional production with better jobs for the future. Government will have a place at the table, as will smart entrepreneurial minds who push ever harder to create the new. And there will be salespeople in the future. They'll be competing against the internet and artificial intelligence to find their place in the mix. Successful salespeople will own a piece of the future. They'll need to zig and zag, to punch and counterpunch, to find their new solid ground. We will all be rookies in the future. But the more we learn about new industries, new discoveries, and the different ways to satisfy customers, the brighter that future can be. Never stop learning.

Lesson learned from Steve Brady

Steve is one of the more interesting people in this book. After suffering through a challenging period in his field, Steve discovered sales in a new industry and he flourished. After a time, he realized he was no longer satisfied and looked to another industry to discover a place to showcase his skills. He wanted more free time and a better lifestyle. He is back at the top of his game, succeeding in a very different industry. He delights customers by going all out. His clients trust Steve and his word. When I first met Steve, he was looking for something better. Today, he is a successful professional, serving multiple markets, while mentoring a new class of sales professionals. He is in this book because he is an example of grit, determination, and the constant search for improvement. He is authentic and true to his values, while always looking to do the best for each and every customer. This is one of his stories:

> "The customer came in, wanting to talk about moving her event to my business. She worked at one of the finest schools in the state, so the opportunity could be large. This event had been held at a grand private club in the area. Because it was so well-regarded, I was surprised that she would want to talk with me. When I asked her why she was considering moving her event, the answer surprised me.
>
> "Ice," she said.
>
> During the previous event, she needed extra ice, so she asked eight people for help. Each one said they were too busy or that it was not their job. During

our conversation, the customer said she was only exploring her options, as the private club had held her event for years. Realizing that price was not going to be a hurdle, I positioned the event at a fair price but added I would also supply unlimited ice. I e-mailed my proposal.

Within five minutes the customer responded. She simply said, "You listened." That event became a very big deal for us. It's a $20,000 event. It has been back now for the past 14 years, and it has turned into a $250,000 account. Because we listened."

Planning

"Great salespeople don't have the ability to feel sorry for themselves."

Barbara Corcoran.

One of the important steps in becoming successful is acquiring a process for the way you present to customers and prospects. It's something that you develop, unique to you and the products you sell. This process becomes your identity in the territory. Besides developing the discipline to execute in front of your customer, it helps to develop logical steps that can lead to a successful conclusion. Your process is you and cannot come from a book or class. Certainly, you can call on mentors to provide counsel, but creating a style becomes part of your brand. Planning is another vital part of your process.

TIME: YOUR MOST PRECIOUS RESOURCE

You will drive your own level of success by the way you manage your calendar. It's your most important tool because time is your most valuable resource. Respect your time and the time of every account and prospect. Know that when a buyer gives you their time, it is a sign of respect both for you and your company.

Here are a few notes from experience: book your appointments 2-3 weeks out, and then confirm 48 hours before the meeting. Many things change and you never want to assume. Be early for every appointment. When there is an issue on your side, even if it means being a few minutes late, contact your buyer and tell them the situation. Walking into an appointment late, without notice, is not acceptable. Treat all time as priceless. As you age, you will understand why. Time is what you provide your organization and your customers. Learn how to squeeze the most out of every hour. They're priceless, but not endless.

PRESENT EVERYTHING, ASSUME NOTHING

As you prepare for your presentation, plan to present your entire product story. Products that are current and available to ship. Unless a buyer has a specific list of the items they want to see, plan to present your full menu. There is value to showing everything you can ship. When you begin to limit your options, you will cost yourself sales. You don't need to think like the buyer. Your job is to present your story with the best reasons to invest in you and your brand. Omitting things, assuming the buyer has no interest can save you time, but potentially cost you as well.

I learned this lesson from a great sales professional very early in my career. He taught me, *never mastermind your customer.* Never assume you know from the start, what they will or won't buy. Continue to show your products until the buyer stops you or asks to review other items in your lineup. Oftentimes, sales reps look at the buyer and their business and create their ideal sales order. Except you are not the decision maker. You are in a place to present and sell all you can. You don't know what's on the buyers' minds, the problems they may have with other suppliers. No doubt, you will only have a short window to present your lineup, so prioritize.

Buyers are always looking to freshen up their stories and change up their business model. You may be there for more reasons than you know. The best buyers are always on the lookout for new and different, so show your entire lineup. You never know how many times you'll hear a "yes."

It's always about credit

Working in an industry that gives customers 30 to 90 days or more to pay an invoice has been extraordinary. Credit makes the business world churn. A continuous, open line of credit has great value in growing an enterprise. The more credit an account has, the more they can buy, stock, and sell. Establishing good credit is critical for every business. It means building a healthy organization, hiring people, and growing.

There are accounts that enjoy good credit and there are other accounts that, well, don't. No order is complete until you've until it has shipped.. New accounts often must pay in advance or as the goods ship.When an account gets into trouble, orders don't ship, reps are kept away, and getting new products is simply not possible.

As you work your territory, know that an open credit line is essential to doing business. Although you're not a bill collector, you have the best relationship with each buyer and their organization. Do what you can to help your company get paid because when invoices are open, you don't get paid. If accounts are on credit hold, you won't be able to present new products or even visit. So don't go after orders where credit is in question. Be aware of who has open credit and who doesn't. Managing your territory means selling to those who are able to pay. So always know the score before you hit the road.

Fit

Your sales manager wants numbers. They want you out in the world, connecting with customers, moving more products. Sliding past the angst and the noise, there are things to consider as you strategize and create your daily calendar:

- Do you have a high-quality list of prospects?
- Are they true candidates for your products?
- Even if they are good prospects, do they have the credit and shelf space?

- What are they offering today that competes directly with your lineup?
- What are their loyalties to other brands, other people?

Because your calendar is your most valuable asset, you want to spend time in front of buyers who are at least willing to move a conversation forward. Whether the order can happen today or later, it's important to spend time with people who have the interest and the capacity to buy what you sell. With high fuel costs, driving to unqualified accounts is not smart, and poor use of your time and resources. But timing is invaluable. Knowing when to reach out and connect to those buyers — at least the ones interested in a conversation — is crucial to creating new accounts. It's important to build a calendar that gets you in front of the right people at the right moments. As you work your territory, face time at the right time is your best course of action.

Be forever ready to adjust

Preparing for any product presentation is important. The detail, structure, questions, and rehearsal each play a part in building your success. You go into every meeting with a series of goals to achieve. In addition to all of the above, you make sure your samples are in order and ready to present. As you prepare, you have your goals in order and your plan. The one thing about preparation is that it's your story, developed by you and your organization. The buyer has their own game plan. Plus, they know the issues that exist beyond your brand, with current sales, inventory levels, and the overall state of their business. The buyer has many product options in their lineup. So the more you can learn before you enter the room, the better prepared you will be to adjust your direction based on new information.

As you prepare, leave space to adjust or pivot away from the script, in order to be current with new information. Alter the questions, structure, and certainly the end goals based on new data. Listening in those first several minutes and being ready to pivot is an important trait of the successful sales pro. Do not go into any meeting with a hard and fast presentation that doesn't leave room for anything the buyer has to say. You may need to hold some things back or scrap the presentation altogether to just listen. Finally, take detailed notes.

YOU CAN ALWAYS IMPROVE

There was a time when top sales professionals latched onto great brands, selling top lines to major accounts. Then they coasted through their career, landing in a warm, soft retirement. Today, no matter your experience or success, every person is vulnerable. Organizations that must reduce headcount or shrink territories will terminate people. Your time with the company or past success may have little relevance as organizations believe they can do more with less.

This is not meant to be an alarm, but it is a call to action. Just as your employer has the opportunity to cut territories, you can also move on and seek a fresh start. No matter your success, resting on a pile of money cannot be a solid goal. Before you decide to move on, you'll want to be prepared. Being up to date about your territory as well as your industry is important. Here are a few suggestions to consider.

- Dig in to find out where your industry is headed.
- Who are the new, up-and-coming organizations?
- Who are the new interesting, industry up and comers?
- What skills are in short supply?
- What skills must you improve in order to better compete?
- How can you grow a more effective network for the changing future?
- How can you turn your current success into a meaningful future?

There will be a need for great sales professionals for a long time to come. In order to work in that future, it's critical to own tomorrow's skills, knowledge, and network. As you age, your contact list ages, too. To remain a sought-after sales pro, you must build a new network of new buyers, managers, and the up-and-coming men and women who will be taking over the landscape. It's essential to prepare for almost everything you do to change or feel different than today.

As Rocky Balboa said: "Father time is undefeated." Unlike athletes, however, sales professionals can continue to excel provided they grow in knowledge, skill, and network. There is no way to succeed tomorrow with the skills and habits of yesterday. Sales professionals will continue to have great opportunities, provided they're prepared when new doors open. Otherwise, that pile of money will continue to shrink. Go to where the future will be to keep the money coming in.

What if everything I'm doing is wrong

As my career grew and I gained more and more responsibility, I realized that mistakes from my desk would be very costly. Thinking about this concern over and over, I came up with a quirky exercise. Although quirky, it proved to be effective as it gave me a very different set of views of the work and potential results. This exercise, which I did once a month, took roughly 30 minutes. I would shut the door to my office, asking not to be disturbed. With a legal pad, I would write down the opposite decision from one I was planning to make about a brand or product. At the top of the page, I wrote the title of this lesson. In one instance, I had to decide on a season-long program with a top supplier which would have meant purchasing hundreds of thousands of dollars, before replenishment, across our locations throughout the organization.

Prior to the final meeting with the supplier, I grabbed my legal pad, writing out the what-ifs of not signing off on the program. It was a smart exercise as it provided ideas of how to produce similar sales and margins, without the huge commitment. I never made that deal, deciding instead to use a few suppliers, minus the major spend.

There were several other examples over the years where I

wanted to confirm my direction. In the majority of cases, I ended up moving forward as planned. This exercise was a validator for me in completing any deal. Buying is a lonely endeavor at times. Arguing the case on paper, with yourself, can be one way to enhance confidence in your approach.

Once I exhausted the questions, I would review each answer, looking for decisions that could be improved. It was an eye-opener. It gave me a way to make decisions by seeing a wider screen. It presented crazy decisions that at least got me to pause, slow down, and make certain of my final path. It made me a better buyer. I used this exercise for many years. How would you respond to this question? How might it change the next three months for you? How might you see things differently? In the end, it's a real exercise for seeing wider, digging deeper, and pausing to make certain the next moves are the best decisions. As a sales professional, you can do this same exercise. Playing out alternatives might provide a better direction or validate you current course. It can work for each side of the desk.

THE SEARCH

There are times you should seek out potential possibilities for change. Although you may not be ready, you at least want to see what's available. This is also a great exercise in judging how you are being treated by your current organization. Being content with your work is no longer a good thing to be; you should be challenged and love your work. And as your success grows, you may find organizations chasing after you. Today, it has been said that 10,000 people per day are retiring. Combine that with the current Great Resignation, and you can imagine the talent shortage that exists. As you begin your search, be certain to know what you're looking for in a new organization.

This is a time to speak with those you trust. Talk to a few trusted buyers and peers, asking what they know about organizations and their programs. If possible, talk to a few sales professionals in other organizations. The grass is not always greener, and you want to learn all you can during the search. Search for the dirt under the fingernails. You want to match up apples with apples looking at any potential opportunity.

Once you have done the search, write out a list of pros and cons on a sheet of paper to see the difference in what you have today versus opportunities elsewhere. Organizations want results, so if they believe you can produce more of what they want, they'll call you. Over my career, I made two disastrous job choices each for money, and title, nothing more. The first poor decision was saying yes to a sales management role. I had interviewed for a local open sales territory. The company came back and offered me the chance to interview for a management job instead, a larger role that involved lots of travel. I took the management role and lasted only two years. At that time in my life, I needed to remain local and on the ground. My second poor choice was accepting a key role hundreds of miles away from my family. My boss, the owner, and I butted heads almost from the start. I took this job for both title and perks. Accepting it was a mistake I realized not too long after the work began. The boss did not care for my "big city attitude," while I was not a fan of being micromanaged. That role lasted far less than two years. Lessons learned, but the hard way.

So before you make any move, list out the pros and cons. You tend to get better offers when organizations do the chasing. As you grow your success, watch and wait. At the same time, a look and a conversation cost little. It is always good to look over the hedges to see where the grass and the offers grow greenest.

Lesson learned: Kevin McClellan

Kevin has developed into a sales superstar. From a slow beginning, he eventually acquired products and brand names that brought forth real success. Over time, Kevin developed a personal style that made it easy for customers to buy. He always makes certain his customers get all they deserve. He continues with the same strategy and work ethic that brought success his way. Today, Kevin not only continues to represent great brands, he manages an entire sales organization — in addition to his day job. He enjoys his work because he loves his profession and his customers. He is a model for managing a territory and building a strong service strategy for each and every customer.

> "Always have a sense of urgency. Back in the 1990s, I received a very nice awards order from one of my accounts. All items arrived in plenty of time for the awards event. I happened to be at this account for a sales call the day these items were unpacked and set up. Everyone on their team agreed the items looked great. I was a happy man.
>
> Fast forward six months and I received a voicemail from the buyer asking me to stop by. When I did, he showed me one of those awards received six months earlier for an event with "Philadelphia" in the title. It was spelled wrong! I was shocked.
>
> I handled the situation right away, shipping replacement awards directly to the homes of each winner. Although I did not think much about this mistake as a major mishap at the time, I realize taking care of this and other issues with a real sense

of urgency helped me to create a strong service reputation. That has continued to pay dividends, as I continue to sell in the same territory. Manage your business, especially when issues pop up. The fault does not matter, the fix is the only thing the customer cares about."

Communications

"Great sales people are relationship builders who provide value and help their customers win."

Jeffrey Gitomer.

This is one of the great assets of the best sales professionals. Knowing how to be a great listener is a vital part of being able to communicate well. Employers are desperately looking for people who know how to be effective one-on-one and in a group. It is a rare skill that provides real opportunities for those who have mastered it. Being able to listen well, present effectively, and understand what the other side wants is a real part of driving success.

PRESENTATION AS THEATER

As a trained speaker, I enjoy getting up in front of an audience. I have no fear of standing in front of strangers, providing a story, heard in a new way. Being a competent speaker, however, did not come naturally. As with any skill, it takes knowledge followed by a lot of practice. A sales presentation, like a speech, takes planning with much practice, in order to move it in front of your customer or prospect.

Besides understanding the product and programs your organization offers, there are other elements you'll want to add to make the presentation work. It's essential to add the best parts of yourself. No buyer wants to hear a lecture about a product.

Your presentation has to feel natural, certainly not rehearsed. The best presentations over my career as a buyer felt like a conversation between friends. The good ones never felt like a business transaction.

As you develop your business, the time in front of the customer is your two-minute drill. It's in that moment that you put all of yourself into the story. The best presentation feels like theater, more like edutainment, not education. It's a little bit of fun combined with knowledge, all with the intent to create or grow a customer. As a great presenter, you need to own the room, show the product, and ask great questions. Developing a top-flight presentation is a must for any sales pro to build a successful, long-term career. Whatever it is that you do well, be certain to add it to the creative mix. Be certain to think theatre each time you plan your next product presentation.

STIRRING THEIR EMOTIONS

Sales is about getting results and walking away with the order. No matter if you sell a basic item or something aspirational, that thing everyone wants to own, you are judged by the numbers. As people spend more time in the sales game, earning more and more money, they begin to keep score through the commission checks. To get there, however, the best reps have a plan. They listen far more than they speak, digging for an opportunity. They understand how to stir the emotions of the buyer through personal stories. They are looking to pique the buyer's interest, to watch their eyes move and see them squirm in the chair. Making the sale is about bringing the buyer over to your side. By observing their facial expressions and body language, the experienced rep gains cues on what to say or do next.

It's vital to enter the room with great energy and enthusiasm. It's important to turn any appointment from a product presentation into an engagement among friends. Selling with excellence is about moving beyond the typical dog and pony show to a human conversation, where two winners exit the time allotted. To get your buyer interested and excited, it is essential to stir their emotions, and yes — to make it personal, between friends.

STIRRING EMOTIONS, PART 2

For many, sales is about creating interest, widening the eyes, and getting the buyer to move. It's about telling engaging stories. Once you perfect your stories, you can get your buyer to pay attention, smile, and understand why they need what you have. Become a good observer and watch for the buying signals that give a green light to proceed. Building sales is as much great observation as anything. It's about seeing the small details that become big opportunities.

LANGUAGE IS IMPORTANT

In any sales presentation, you want to end with a positive conclusion: walking away with a sizable order. To get to that end means understanding where you are at any point. In my years as a buyer, I saw many reps talk and talk and talk with no summary. There was no plan and I was losing interest by the second.

These meetings ended up with no transaction, or maybe a small fill-in order. It's essential to know where you stand at every point in your presentation. Has the buyer heard you? Have they received the message as presented? There are points in every presentation to stop, ask questions or even go for a conclusion. Be always on point, no matter the relationship you have with the buyer. Choose your words carefully.

It's said that people retain only 20% of what is spoken. So be certain to double down on those points essential to a sale. Buyers are busy and constantly bombarded with noise and interruption. Finding the right words can create more sales. Be specific with your language. It's not about using ten-dollar words; it's not about being smart. It's about using the best words to persuade your buyer to say yes. Emphasize critical points and ask for the order. Never assume your message was received without asking questions.

COMMUNICATIONS

The ability to convey your message and get to Yes is your main objective. Communicating your message in the fewest words is more critical than ever. Having your message received every time is the secret sauce of the profession. With five generations of people now in the workforce, being able to communicate with both younger and more experienced buyers is an essential skill. You may have appointments on the same day with buyers from two different generations. Being able to convey your story to a 26-year-old at 10:00, followed by a 67-year-old at 2:00 is a challenge, yet one seen more frequently. It's an art to be able to sit down with a wide variety of buyers, providing just the right message to create an order and a customer.

As a sales professional, you have many tools in your toolbox. Communications — the ability to build successful professional relationships — is at the top of what you should work to perfect. This is the key to all you want to achieve in your career. You need to know your product inside out, as well as your organization. When you get in front of your buyer, make the conversation simple, friendly, and easy. No matter what you're selling, position the conversation to be on a personal level. In the end, friends will buy from friends.

Words

As a new buyer I didn't possess a great bag of words. In fact, I had a poor vocabulary at that time. When I sat down with a sales rep, or worse, their manager, I felt intimidated. Sure, I held the power and the purchase order, but it didn't feel very right or equal. They knew more than I did. They spoke better than I did. Being in that situation once too often made me realize the only way to be better was to get better. Eventually, my goal was to be the best buyer in my industry. Although I never reached that summit, I became someone who would own the room, no matter who else was at the table.

As a sales professional, it's one thing to have essential knowledge necessary to create a sale. It's another level to speak in a way that will move your buyer to action. Knowing your organization, your industry, and the fine details of your products are all important. Presenting the necessary information in a way the buyer understands is the real 7-figure skill.

Once you have the skills, you gain the confidence. Once you

have the skills and confidence, all roads will be open to you. Knowing what to say and how to say it are the skills that will pay dividends for as long as you're in the profession. If sales is all about monetizing skills, then understanding how to deliver your words is the 7-figure asset for your tool kit.

Written words win the day

The "he said, they said" argument is as old as the human race. In any conversation, some points are remembered, others get lost. This lesson was a game-changer for me. Certainly, we want to trust people. That's what good business is all about. But motivations change, pressures move about, and what was said may no longer apply. It's absolutely critical to keep clear notes in every meeting. From the notes in the original meeting to each and every follow-up, having written notes to reference is far better than trying to remember the exact points stated by either side.

There were several times, as a young buyer, when I placed an order based on what I had heard. When the execution was far different than what I had remembered, I began taking notes of every supplier meeting. After each meeting, I summarized the notes and forwarded them to all in attendance. That was me, the buyer. You, as the sales pro, should own that task. You want clarity for every meeting. You want everyone to be and remain on the same page. So make notes of the critical comments, as well as points of agreement. Relying on memory is a poor plan that will ultimately result in misunderstandings and incorrect orders with costly results. No sales pro should trust what is heard without the benefit of written notes and follow-up.

Now, in my professional life, there are no meetings without note-taking. I want to be sure of what was said, clear on the next steps for each side. After any meeting, I ask that notes are shared so all are in agreement. No one wants a congenial meeting to turn sour because of a misunderstanding. When you take and share good notes, you build clarity and trust and enable agreements to move forward.

GETTING IT RIGHT MATTERS

As technology changes, the number one sought-after skill for new hires is excellent communication skills. Timely, clear communication is essential to growing relationships and business. Many salespeople take information for granted and assume several next steps. Over my career, I have learned that even one missing step in the order chain can create great damage to an order or a business relationship. As a sales rep bringing an order home, why leave anything to chance? It's essential to connect the dots to assure the order can be approved and shipped. When something goes wrong, go back to the people involved and examine the process.

It is vital leaving nothing to chance, especially with a new account or a new member of your team. Building a winning process for each account will enable them to feel more comfortable with you and your company. Many people may touch an order along the process, so be sure that process is intact and that every team member is working to move your orders out the door. Take the time to communicate with everyone. Build respect and clarity within the team. The more the team works together, the faster the orders can move out the door.

INFORMATION, INFORMATION, INFORMATION

If career success is built upon a foundation of timely information, then intense listening is the path to that success. Critical information about buyers, accounts, and competitors will help you navigate your business in a way that eliminates wasted steps, errors, and going down one-way streets.. Good questions will help uncover the necessary detail to build relationships and trust. Once you have the important answers, build a file for every account and buyer. Creating these files may feel like a burden at first, but the information will help build your business.

In my experience, too many sales reps just do not listen. Or they may listen, but not well enough to get the critical answers they need. It takes intentional practice to become a good listener. The better the questions, the better the answers. Many reps get the easy answers but fail to dig deeper and pull out information about competitive brands, inventory, or credit issues. Good questions and patience win the day. Once you have the information to move ahead, you'll know where to push and how hard. Sales is not a race. It can take time and patience to reach your destination. Don't rush. Try never to take a small, simple order. Spend the time to research, question, and compile the information that will help you maximize your business.

Connecting the dots

Because buyers can now access information online, sales is now about consulting, timely follow-up, and a specific service strategy. It's about pulling the story together and connecting the dots to ensure the buyer understands the plan, product, and programs you hope to execute. Some reps talk and talk without a plan or summary in mind. It's important to slow down, listen, and take in the information. Every detail can help connect the dots. Don't ask yes and no questions, but questions that require detail. Each meeting should be an exercise in connecting the dots, in pursuit of gaining long-term benefits with every account.

Always define, never assume

In looking to create success, you need to be certain your message is being received by your buyers. Yes, information is available digitally, and while today's sales pros don't have to carry heavy product catalogs into meetings, you still have to customize the information. Don't assume your buyer knows the important details, especially when it comes to program options, terms, pricing, and other decision making points. It's the finer points that will help you draw the conversation to a successful close. Expecting the buyer to be totally up on your brand and product story is a mistake that can cost you. Always take a few minutes to understand where your buyer stands and how you should proceed.

Touching base

Staying connected with your buyers is essential, whether you're new to the job or a long-term veteran; it's important to have a file on every account and buyer to capture important details: Things they like and information about their life outside of work. How often to contact them. Whether they prefer a call, text, or email. If you're not sure, ask.

It's not just about building business, but building friendships. Touching base just to say hello, to ask how they're doing is a smart move. It doesn't happen often. When you reach out just to connect, without any hidden agenda, you come off as someone interested in more than a purchase order.

Knowing your buyers and staying connected will pay dividends over time. As a key account manager, when I called only to touch base, I received an order, six out of 10 calls. When you stay in view, you build connection. Get to know your buyers' likes and preferences; it all matters.

STAY CONNECTED

The first priority of the sales professional is to sell. There's nothing tricky about that. If the rep is not writing orders, who will? Sometimes, a buyer gets upset so a supplier gets dropped. Sometimes, buyers simply rotate suppliers from year to year. You might end up losing an account through no fault of your own.

No matter the reason for the change, it's important to remain connected. Unless it was a 5-star mistake, there is every chance that a buyer will restart a conversation. It may take time, but it can happen. Unless you are banished for life, never give up on an account or buyer. No territory is so large that the sales rep can erase an account from their system.

Whether you are out because of a mistake or simply a change, stay in touch. Reach out after some time and invite the buyer to lunch. Your mission is always to work your way back into their favor.

Being chosen: What is your secret sauce?

During my career, I have known thousands of sales professionals. They were from all over the spectrum of achievement, confidence, and work ethic. The best reps I have known over my career owned the following traits:

- They executed.
- They knew their daily mission.
- They knew their goals with every sales call.
- They had no wasted motion in their presentation.
- They had real confidence in their own knowledge and ability.
- They each understood, they were working for their buyer.
- They listened, making their buyer feel important.

Yes, these reps were focused on income, but as the result of the effort. Sales reps come and go all the time, especially now that the Boomer generation is aging out, and younger generations take on their roles.

What about you? Why would a sales manager interview or hire you? What is your secret sauce? What will you do for the organization? What will you do for the territory and buyers? You have skills. Do you know what they are? Can you articulate them during a job interview? Before you get to see the buyer, you must sell to the sales manager why you are the best candidate to take the territory to another level.

It might make sense to talk to a few of the great sales reps before they leave for good. That would be a great use of your time. Know your value. Understand and be able to sell that value. The question on the minds of every sales manager is this: "what's in it for me?" They want to know why they should hire you. Practice until you believe in the answer. Then prepare to do all you said you will do and more.

Lesson learned from Scott Smith

After many years on the road, working as a sales rep, I moved to the management side. I joined one of the prominent brands in my industry. One week I was working with one of the sales reps in their territory. On reviewing an account we were about to visit, the rep told me it had been tough to establish a solid relationship due to the fact this account kept changing buyers.

> Scott has been in the sales game for most of his career. Moving from sales rep to sale management was a natural for Scott. Moving from sales to management was a progression made easy due to Scott's experience, demeanor and skill set. He is a big-picture professional, one that is as comfortable building brands, as he is building territories.
>
> After some time, my rep gained her trust. They have since established a good working relationship. He has become a person to provide feedback ever since that first meeting. The brand has established a solid account due to our desire to help and support a new buyer. We were more interested in long-term results, versus an order during that first meeting.

Execution

> "The questions you ask are more important than the things you could ever say."
>
> Thomas Freese.

Execution is the most important part of business. After the conversations, the planning, and scheduling, it is about getting it done. Sit in a crowd of salespeople and you quickly learn who talks a good game and who wins more than their share. There are as many ways to win as there are industries. It comes down to being liked and trusted, and then writing the order. You know you are succeeding after you have written your fourth or fifth order with the customer. Execution is about getting things done.

FACE-TO-FACE

We live and sell in a very different world. Different from the days before the internet, even different from before the pandemic. Just think, it was only 2019 when the sales professional had to make an appointment, sharpen up the samples, fill up the gas tank, and head out to see the buyer face-to-face. There is no substitute for being face-to-face, whether you're a buyer or a seller. Being able to work directly with a buyer, observing their buying signals is critical to creating more sales and long-term relationships.

The best sales reps love being on stage, showcasing new products or programs. They bring energy and enthusiasm not experienced in a virtual setting. Sales reps get excited about new products and opportunities. They want to instill that enthusiasm into their buyers.

Take away the ability to present face-to-face and many reps feel lost, unable to grab the energy required to excite the buyer into action. Today, however, there is a whole new ball game with options that weren't acceptable or available prior to March 2020. At that moment, every company had to change the way they did business. They had no choice.

Business went forward, although many limped into their next phase as every organization had to adjust. Virtual presentations through Zoom, Microsoft Teams, or Google Meet became the accepted choices to connect, present, and purchase the next order. It's important to take the temperature of your buyers, asking if they prefer to meet face-to-face or virtually. My belief is that, for new product presentations and the new season, face-to-face should be your direction.

For checking in and account maintenance, being able to meet virtually will save you time and money, while still letting you achieve the reason for the meeting. Always think face-to-face, while making certain you know how each of your buyers wants to connect. Offering no option to the buyer is not a good decision.

"Why should I buy?"

When I was a buyer, I was presented with hundreds and hundreds of new programs and products. For the rep it was all about the yes. The reps knew I spent a great deal of money, and they were looking to capture a portion of that budget. The presentations ranged from very rehearsed and structured to general conversations where the rep was trying to get a quick Yes.

In preparing to write this section, I thought back over many of the presentations. It became evident that many of the reps did not provide me with enough detail to make a decision. And most never asked about my inventory levels or overall business concerns. Did I have a need? Did I have an opening to buy? I realized that some reps cared little about my concerns or my business. Many often skipped to the last page, just looking to secure a quick order.

It's important to remember that we all have a boss. Not only are buyers trying to do their jobs well, they're looking to stay in the job doing what they love. No buyer is going to give out unnecessary orders. They're not going to risk their current situation or future by tossing a gift to any salesperson. Certainly, your role is to present products and programs that can work for this account and show how your story is better than your competitors. Until the buyer is convinced and has the shelf space, they will remain in the undecided camp. Buyers are not in place to help salespeople reach their targets. When the buyer understands your motives, products, and program, it is time to move forward. Until they do, you have some work yet to do.

The appointment

To most sales professionals, the presentation is the thing. To them, it is theatre. The chance to put their skills on display. It is the best part of the role. Before the rep arrives, prepared to roll out programs and samples, there is that other thing that must come first. This might be the toughest part of a great job. If you are contacting current, open accounts, there is only the matter of finding a date on the calendar. If you are reaching out to prospects or inactive accounts, getting an appointment can be a challenge.

Buyers get comfortable with brands that work and reps that understand their organization. They trust the routine. They trust the sales professionals and brands within a small circle. When they're asked to step out and meet with a new rep or new brand, red lights go off. They don't understand why they would meet and review a new supplier. Although all buyers should remain on your radar, some will take work to get onto your calendar.

In my experience, the better way to connect to a prospect is through a phone call, never a text or email. An introduction from another sales rep already doing business with the buyer may help open the door. Buyers are generally guarded against people they do not know. It's important to not give up; it's part of the work.

Once an appointment is set, don't count your commission dollars. The first meeting is about getting to know the buyer, while the buyer has the opportunity to understand you and your story. It's a first date: a simple meetup. It is also a time to secure that critical

2nd appointment in order to establish a potential go-forward plan. Take time out of each week to make the calls. No appointments, no new accounts. Although the top 20% of accounts produce 80% of business for a supplier — that's the Pareto Principle, or 80/20 rule — acquiring new accounts and greater distribution will forever be a vital part of the role, and the daily mission of every sales manager.

What points have I missed

Listening is such a vital skill in sales. During any presentation, it is important to follow it both in your mind and ears. In many cases, a rep has so much to cover, they can easily forget a key point or important question. It is important to remember what was discussed and what was missed. Remembering the points that stoked the buyer's interest are critical to note. Before you summarize, go back over the presentation in your head. Did you miss a point from your presentation? Before you finish, review review your stated presentation. Be sure your message was received.

Problem solver

As a sales rep you are a professional. You were hired to sell and create long-term customers. These are the facts. An additional idea, duty actually, is the fact that in addition to writing orders and creating customers, you are managing a series of accounts over an entire territory. When an account has a problem, an issue, it is your job to solve the problem and relieve their pain. When I was a buyer, I looked to the local sales rep or territory manager to apply their assets to the problem. Poor communication is an ongoing shortfall in just about every industry. These lapses in communication can cause any number of missteps that can result in ill feelings, less business, or worse, the end of a relationship.

Problems will vary from we didn't get the memo, you never told me, or that wasn't in the presentation. Of course, there are dozen of reasons why problems pop up, causing potential rifts between an account and a supplier.

No matter how it happens, the idea is not to push blame back and forth. The specific focus must be on finding a solution as quickly as possible. You'll want to eliminate the problem from your buyer's plate. As the suppliers' representative, you want to quickly get to and identify the issue. As the individual closest to the customer, you are the best person to find a solution. Take the same sense of urgency into solving a problem as you would in shipping a large order. Ignoring or pushing off an issue is not good business.

It may cause the buyer to pause your relationship, or worse, cut it off altogether. What other leverage does a buyer have? When an account is hurting, run to the problem. Find out the cause, communicate a fix to the buyer and your team, then move on to fixing the issue. Anyone can take an order, but not every sales rep is willing to jump in and fix what is broken. Buyers admire the fixer.

THE OTHER SIDE OF THE SALE

I have known many sales reps that believe their work was finished once they received an order. They want the product shipped on time and in full, but other than that, they believe they're done.

As a former buyer, I can tell you that's not how the other side thinks. Buyers believe the salesperson should own a significant piece of the transaction. Although buyers do not expect the rep to move the product onto the floor themselves, they do expect them to provide support in the areas of product training, marketing, and presentation advice.

Certainly, the more the buyer's team knows about the product, the more success can be had by both sides. The buyer's sales team will be much more confident about the product and their ability to sell it. As the account rep, your need to know and understand your buyers' expectations; a one-size-fits-all service plan will not work. Knowing their expectations is essential in building long-term customers. Every buyer expects support in moving your products to their customers. Knowing how this applies to each of your buyers will bring you better relationships and a better reputation that leads to even more sales.

EXECUTION, THE LESSON

Know what matters to your sales manager and to every buyer. When it comes to execution, it is all about the people above that will enable you to win the race. Execution is why you wake up every morning. Creating new orders and customers is the caffeine that enables you to build your business, build wealth, and create success.

The role of the rep is to write business and create long-term customers. Execution is the key for those who want to succeed. One of the important lessons here is to manage the things you want to do versus the things you must do.

There's the preparation for an upcoming meeting, including practice working with your samples. There is the follow-up after every meeting. In addition, you must ensure every order has been sent in with all information thoroughly checked. You know maintenance, preparation, and follow-up are an integral part of every meeting and sale. There are many chores to accomplish in any week as a sales professional. The secret is to manage the time spent on the maintenance so you have all the time you need to visit your customers. A busy week should never keep you from the reasons you are in the role.

WORKING WITH DIFFICULT CUSTOMERS

During your career you will get to work with all types of personalities. Understand that buyers are under a lot of pressure themselves, just like you. They must pick products their customers want to buy and choose the right levels of inventory. And that must lead to sales with strong gross margins for their organization.Unless they own the business, your buyers have a boss. The job for any buyer is a juggling act where both the end customer and the organization must win. Any other results just don't matter.

During the first half of my buying career, I was not a very nice person. I was tough. I felt the pressure and generally took it out on the sales rep and their management. There is no doubt I was fighting for my customer each and every day, looking to provide both products and value. No doubt, I could have handled myself differently. It was my quest to make certain we were building the business, making money, and helping customers. I was tough, but I was fair. In addition, many sales reps made a great deal of money from my sales orders. Eventually, I got smarter, I got softer, and I understood that in most cases, both sides wanted the same results.

You will face all types of buyers. It's important to always be professional, understanding your products and programs. To have confidence and to never feel intimidated. The more you know, the more respect you will be given. When you meet with a difficult buyer, be on time, smile, and present.

Remember, you represent an organization and its people, so remain focused and calm. If things get a bit rough, call a break and walk to the restroom. Remember, it's a transaction, not a war.

Some buyers are easy and welcoming. Others will treat you as the enemy who is holding their pot of gold. Always be a pro, and always be consistent. Every buyer deserves your best across the board. If a buyer gets too far out of line, you may need to walk away and allow them to cool down. There will be difficult buyers in your career. It's important to know your story, do your job well, and always respect the people and the situation. Always take the higher ground.

MISSING NUMBERS

If you are in sales, you have sales goals. Every sales professional and organization has a series of targets. They are the reason we all wake up in the morning. Because I have been part of developing goals through the years, I generally found myself scratching my head as I walked away, wondering how senior leadership signed off on the final budgets. There seemed to be more hope and wishing instead of goals based on historical numbers.

Nevertheless, there are goals in several categories to be attacked and achieved. Targets for the month, quarter, and year. Once you have your goals, you'll think about them daily, while speaking about them often with your sales manager.

A sales organization lives or dies with its numbers. During my time in business, selling both B-to-C and B-to-B, I can only recall budgets being reduced a few times, due to extraordinary circumstances.

On the other hand, goals seem to be made of helium. They tend to travel north. Many times they are increased when leadership senses any upward trend. What happens however when the economy is poor, the product lineup is mature, and out of sizzle? What do you do when things are bad and you're not writing orders with any consistency? What happens when it's hard to book appointments? Here are some thoughts on what to do in tough times:

- Talk to your sales manager. Develop an action strategy together.

- Meet with your mentor to gain an outside perspective.

- Spend time with your best customers, asking tough questions about the industry.

- Spend alone time, developing ideas and going thoroughly through your numbers.

- Review and improve your presentation. Base it on current need and circumstances.

- Develop sales promotional ideas, presenting the best ones to your manager.

- Do not get down, but continue to think about who can buy what you sell.

- Look to spend more time with prospects or inactive accounts.

- Work on your energy and enthusiasm. You are a professional.

Every organization has tough times. If there are goods to sell, the organization has to find new ideas and new programs to entice the customer base. Maintaining connections with your customers, especially the top 20%, is vital to building sales when times improve. Look for ways to create new and different promotions that build interest. Never give up. You have customers who like you and trust you. Treat them like superstars, no matter the volume in the moment. When numbers are down, it's time to think about the next great promotion.

Using information

Today, we are in the early stages of the digital transformation, with a lot of data at our fingertips, more than we can use on most days. Don't get too hung up on the data. Data managed well can help you push forward, avoid potholes, and better manage your daily activities. Within the data, there are details that matter to your organization and your customers.

The more unencumbered time spent with customers means there are opportunities to develop better relationships. Focus daily on the major items of your business, leaving the minor, non-essential items to the end of the day.

Understanding what is happening with each account and the products they purchase yields important data that will help you manage your next call. Knowing the details about each account may also provide ideas about additional sales and brand extensions to present. There is always new data to review, so pulling out what can be most helpful is the secret. Getting too deep into the data weeds only wastes time and plays havoc with your priorities. Building a concise report can help you spend the right amount of time reviewing the data most important to your efforts. Helping your customers build their success is the larger mission. Using data to get there is the solution. If you need help with it, find someone to support your efforts, making certain you continue to manage your time with the customer in mind.

Do the stuff that matters

There are many people who get things done, completing task after task. Although they move through a series of to-do lists, they achieve little, as it relates to what their customers expect. Success is not about completing tasks, it's about achieving the items that are important to your organization and your customers. These achievements should enable you to hit your monthly and quarterly numbers.

Build your to-do list the day before, listing the five or six most critical items. Be sure to prioritize the list from top to bottom. Once you do the first one, the next item becomes your new number one priority. Everyone says they are busy these days, but busy doing what? You have a series of people anticipating your efforts: your sales manager, customers, and your organization. When your time is spent in those three arenas, you're on your way to a successful year. It's all a matter of doing the right stuff that makes the difference.

SUPPLY CHAIN PAIN

We work in a global economy. Parts and products are made all over the planet. It doesn't matter the industry or organization, most products today arrive by ship, long before they hit the highway to your customers' doors. The system worked fairly well for decades, until the global pandemic. It put a halt to the manufacture, assembly, and delivery of goods everywhere. No one saw it coming, so no one was prepared. It takes years and years to recreate an industry close to home, so the world had to suffer through what became a serious supply chain problem.

As a salesperson, you are at the other end of this chain. You and your organization have waited for ships to arrive, to be offloaded, and loaded onto trucks. It has been a continuous hiccup of product delays, shortages, and missed orders.

In the end, it's out of your control. The lesson here is to be honest and upfront with the information you do know. It's OK to lose an order, it's never OK to lose an account. This is happening to both large and small brands, so look to be a solution for your customers. Search for ways to help. Be in the fight with your customers. Mostly, work to get new information and share it with your customers. Try to be a continuous asset as everyone works through these unprecedented times. Be a solution provider today to sell more tomorrow.

NEVER GO ROGUE

As a sales professional you represent an organization, maybe more than one. Whether you're a company rep working for one vendor or an independent rep selling multiple brands, you're the front-line connection to the buyer. As their representative in the territory, it's important to always color within the lines. When it comes to pricing, terms, and any other promises, stay within the framework of the company programs, unless your manager has given you written approval to go above and beyond.

Work with your manager to carry out what you can and can't do. If products are not available, be upfront and honest. Never assume your manager can pull off a miracle in getting products for a customer. If an account demands better pricing, better terms, or a higher allocation, pass those requests to your manager. Your role is to sell, while the sales manager's is to tweak approved pricing or programs. Have them make these decisions while you stay out of the line of fire.

Do all you can for your customer, but never go rogue. Never make a decision that may haunt you down the road. Be the ambassador for your customers, but don't make decisions above your pay grade as most will rarely work out in your favor.

People

"Do what you fear most and you control fear."
Tom Hopkins.

In order to win big in sales, it is almost a prerequisite that you like people. Putting people first, before you jump into the presentation is an important part of creating and then building relationships. Whether on a call or in person, a familiar conversation about the buyer and their family helps to create a bond that can get stronger over time. I have learned that connecting through conversation is the richer path to success rather than simply asking for the business. Building friends will help you earn more than you might ever imagine. As you start each day, plant the idea in your mind that people are first on your agenda. They have problems, deadlines, and life issues. Including empathy first will help you gain support over time. Think first about building relationships. After that, do everything you can to build a strong business together.

Your buyer also bleeds

Buyers are real people. They can be a leader within an organization, but they have a very specific set of duties, different from the rest of the management team. Unless they're the boss, they have a boss. They work each day to provide products that sell as quickly as possible with good margins. They work hard to make the best product decisions.

Every once in a while, however, they will stumble, picking

products that just won't sell. The smart sales pro is always on their side, playing the role of advocate, friend, and supporter. When mistakes happen, people sometimes want to talk through the issue, seeking out advice and a few minutes to talk.

It makes sense to become that ear, to be someone more than the local territory manager. Conquering your world is important, but knowing when to step back and become an advocate can be even more important.

The buyer role is a lonely one. When a tough situation occurs, the boss is not always the person the buyer might want to speak with in that moment. Talking through a mistake may be a good way to secure a fix for the future. There are times to put the order pad away and just listen. This is the moment the salesperson earns more than commission; they earn their stripes by building a strong relationship. Sales reps will come and go but friends will remain. It's about being present, understanding, and not taking sides.

As we get older, we realize that every person walks through their day with a unique set of challenges. No one is immune. Understand your buyers beyond the size of their business and the number of orders written. Look at your territory, not only as a place to secure, but as a place where people make mistakes and might need a friend.

Respect

Respect is an important value to bring into your sales meetings. There will be people we do not agree with or just may not like. That's something we can all understand. There were many people throughout my career who rubbed me the wrong way. These were people I would not want to spend time with outside the workplace.

At the same time, I decided very early in my management career that I would respect every person I met and/or worked with. Having sincere respect is vital to building professional relationships. There's nothing more important than having respect for your customer. That includes: being prepared, being early, ready to answer most questions that come up during a meeting. It also includes respecting the buyers' time and keeping your phone off and out of view.

Succeeding in sales means getting the people thing right. Buyers expect you to be prepared and know about your products and programs. Because the buyer has already been on your website and dug into your catalog, you need to come in with more. Bring some information the buyer can't find through a simple web search. Respect shows itself when you're ready to present and work with the buyer as they expect. Treat each buyer as they want to be treated. When you show respect and care for your buyers, you're paying a high compliment.

Mentors

Selling can be tough. It takes time, patience, thick skin, and the ability to hear "No" more times than you can count to endure over the long term. No matter if you work for a company or are an independent rep, the world will not roll out the red carpet for you every time you enter a business. It can take a great deal of magic some days to turn a "No" into a "Yes." Even though you have a sales manager, there is a very lonely feeling every time a rejection pops up. It can take some extraordinary support to wrestle with the tough days. It takes a mentor.

A mentor is a man or woman who knows something about your industry, something about sales, and a great deal about you. They carry the professional scars, earned over years of failure and achievement. Good mentors come with the résumé of success and the willingness to support.

The mentor will know the mentee. They will not know all the answers. They will, however, know the important questions to ask during your relationship. A mentor is a volunteer. A person who wants to help and support you. They want you to succeed and will bring their experience to bear. Regardless of your age or experience level, find someone who can act as your mentor. In the end, the best mentors are priceless.

Leadership

> "You can have anything in life you want, if you just help other people get what they want."
>
> Zig Ziglar.

Any success carries with it some form of leadership. Even an independent salesperson brings skills that can help their buyer in ways beyond fulfilling orders. Succeeding in sales means you relate well to people. It includes the ability to ask great questions, all while looking for ways to help support the buyer and their organization. Leadership does not require a team to execute the required skills. It is about how to represent yourself, conduct your efforts, and service your customers. Leadership is as much about being a true professional as it is driving a team to victory. Consultative selling is as much about leadership as it is about sales. Setting the proper tone with customers is important. Creating and meeting expectations is a true sign of leadership.

CONSULTATIVE SELLING

Selling is vastly different from the days of sales reps in station wagons. It's no longer about bringing information to the buyer. It's about searching for ways to serve each individual better in the ways that make sense for their business.

Because of the internet, e-commerce, and even big-box retailing, selling today is more about advising, coaching, and supporting. It's all about the interest of the buyer and the account. You want your buyers all to reach the same result, but how you arrive there is based on their individual needs and preferences.

Being successful means understanding the specific needs of each account. It's so much more than knowing your products and programs. It's about being close to the people, understanding their needs, and responding with a sense of urgency. Advising customers means being the expert in your company and its products. It is also about listening intently in order to help your buyers make the best possible decisions. When you gain the status of advisor, you become a trusted part of the buyer's circle. A trusted person is more than just a sales rep. Help your buyers achieve their goals and watch your success soar.

Managing expectations

There are many people who have expectations of you and your work, including your manager, organization, buyers, and members of your corporate team. It's essential to work toward their expectations. To be sure you're on the correct path, compare notes, to ensure you're on the same page. If some of the expectations are too high, you'll want to see how you can reset to something more realistic. Meeting expectations requires both parties to agree before the game begins.

Managing everyone's expectations is a skill that will take you a long way. It will help you acquire more orders, grow those orders, and maintain business relationships when the economy slows. Continue to search for information from your community. Doing consistent walkthroughs into your customers' businesses will bring you new information each time. Work to remain on top of the story. When you also provide information about your business to your buyers, you secure a place ever closer to the front of the line.

Spend time with willing leaders

A mistake I made early in my career was always keeping my head down, working hard, and not connecting to the veterans who could help me smooth out the bumpy road ahead. As a young manager,

I thought I was the smart person in the room. Boy, did I have a lot to learn! That was my ego talking. The organization was growing and being at the top made me feel like I had something to do with it. I wish I'd had the listening skills I picked up much later in my career. I could have avoided a great many gaffes. No matter where you are in your career or how old you are, seek out the leaders in your field who can help you grow. Smart people who can give you a much wider view of that ladder you want to climb.

Seek out those who are willing to sit down and spend time talking about the business. Try to find a group of industry leaders willing to give you time and attention. No one succeeds alone. Set up meetings throughout the year, in both the good times and the bad times.

Having conversations with successful people who have done what you want to do can provide an amazing boost. The adrenaline alone is worth the price of the lunch. Experienced people can provide suggestions from real life and share the important dos and don'ts that you might only learn through daily trial-and-error. Spending time with successful people can save you months or even years of missteps and struggles. Be humble: create a list and ask smart people for some time.

LIVE A DAY IN YOUR BUYER'S SHOES

The buyer has the dream job. They get to go to events, trade shows. and conferences to see what's new and different in their industry. They then get to spend other people's money to buy inventory. They make many independent decisions, based on their experience and feel for what will work. They travel all throughout the land in the name of sales and profit. Sounds great right? Buying is fun — I enjoyed it most days.

There is that other side, of course: stress, pressure, and many mistakes. The buyer has both a boss and an audience. The boss has several expectations, based on sales and profits, while the audience wants always to see what is new, different, cool, and fun. Buying is constant: If they're not working on the next project, they're thinking about suppliers to add or drop, goods to mark down, and other things that get in the way of a restful life outside of the office.

Living in the buyer's shoes means

- Having real empathy for the work.
- Understanding that the buyer has many sales reps and suppliers to choose from.
- Looking not to be a sales rep but a partner, one who will listen.
- Understanding that inventory in stock may prevent you from receiving an order today.
- Becoming a partner, interested in success as a whole, not only for your brand and product menu.

Having an empathetic position for your buyer will put you in a very different place. You can wind up working together to grow sales and margins. It begins by walking in your buyer's shoes, feeling what they experience before they write your order. Become the partner there to help them build their success.. The more the buyer can trust you, the more business you will do together.

ANGER

People get mad. A lot. Sales reps cannot ship their orders, so they become angry. Buyers cannot get delivery, and they become angry too. Managing that anger becomes an important professional skill. You may jump in your van tomorrow and get cut off several times before your first appointment, but before you go into it, you must put on a happy face because your buyer doesn't care about your driving challenges. And there are countless reasons why you might become angry with buyers, team members, managers, or the human race in general. But this is not about whether you get angry. It's about managing and hiding any anger you feel before you connect with anyone professionally.

We all know people who wear their attitude on their faces. You know exactly how the next 15 minutes will go when you see the look on the buyer's face; you can't have that same angry look when you enter the room. You can't do anything but be the nice person in the room, improving the mood, moving quickly to the reason for the visit.

Whether you remain a sales professional or move into management, you will need to manage and overcome your anger. If something does flare you up, it's important to never return an angry text with an angry response. Never respond to any kind of angry communication in the moment. Instead, you need to think of the big picture, to step far away, and to do nothing.

Work through the anger. If a response is required, do it the next day. Never allow a situation or mood to jeopardize an order, a customer, or an account. Think the situation through, including the outcome you want to see. The next day, put together a response that leads to a solution. Anger spent never makes a situation better. Walk away, think through the entire issue, and then come back the next day. Space and a bit of air can be the best remedies.

Relationships

> "All you need is the plan, the road map, and the courage to press on to your destination."
>
> Earl Nightingale.

Creating and building professional relationships is critical to your professional success. Having a contact list filled with successful men and women is a must for anyone looking to become more than average. There will be times people on your list will help you connect to the next great customer or help you find a new job. These valuable people will also reach back, looking for your help or advice when detours come their way. Developing relationships with successful people can provide much smoother travel on your trip to the top.

IT'S ABOUT PEOPLE

From the time you receive the job offer, you'll want to develop the business and territory. That means building relationships with everyone in your community, beginning with the top accounts. Building success as a sales professional means building longevity into your plan. By developing relationships, you not only show others what you're willing to do for them, you show that you are real, authentic, and ready to work hard for their business.

Create a file on every account and include the type of distribution, the number of locations, buyer information, and all other critical points about the account. List the likes of the buyers, including their favorite hobbies.

As a buyer, I appreciated it when a few sales reps provided me access to their hockey tickets. When they offered, I always bought two. My son was young at the time and hockey was his thing. That access for me created a stronger bond with the sales reps.

Was I happy to hear from them? You bet, almost anytime. When you develop relationships that go beyond the sales call and the order, you break down barriers by developing friendships. Always keep in mind that understanding and appreciating your buyers is a top priority. Business is personal because it involves people working with people. When you decided to get into sales, you decided to work diligently to understand people. The better your relationships, the more frequent the appointments, the higher your average sale, and the greater your annual income. Long before you get to the goals or the products, it's always about the people.

Your community

Over a career, we touch many people. From the beginning, we are building the network we will nurture and connect to for years. Early on, you may have just a few people in your community. But if you make this a proactive program, you can grow a solid network surprisingly fast. You will have multiple types of people in your community: buyers, prospects, industry leaders, other sales reps, managers, and members of your internal team. As your career grows, so should your network.

Adding years means adding events. There, you'll have access to new people and leaders you want to get to know. Recognizing, nurturing, and staying connected to your network is so important. The best information about new jobs and opportunities comes from your network.

There is always a group of leaders to be found. These people know about the people, opportunities, and changes that occur, long before much of the world does. These people can help make your success, so stay in touch and connect often, helping and supporting them as you do. If nothing else, just reach out to keep the lines of communication open. Staying in touch can give access to opportunities that may never appear to those outside your network.

Your community will shrink and grow over time. Relationships are like financial accounts: They work in two directions. Savings requires deposits before there can be a withdrawal. Nourish your important relationships. Put time and energy into them before you consider making a withdrawal.

SUCCESS TRAIT #1

We all want to be insiders, to be invited to the adult table. Gaining access to the people that make a difference will set you apart from the crowd. Being an insider can move you from doing well to becoming an elite player. Being invited to the best accounts and biggest opportunities will position you for a very successful future. If A-list buyers like you, they'll connect you to their peers. Selling to top accounts creates a book of business not available to most people.

Being liked means doing the things each day that helps everyone see you at your best. Talk with and respect every person at an account, not just the buyer. Splash that smile on early and keep it fresh throughout your day. Be on purpose each day. Find your path to being the most liked person in the territory and reinforce it. No matter how long it takes, work to be the person people always want to do business with. Besides the smile and charm, do everything you can to do right by each account. Proper execution, done on time, will move you onto center stage. Being liked is not only a nice advantage, it's the most valuable thing you can do.

EMPATHY ALWAYS

Every person you know walks through life with their own challenges and unique baggage. The weight can be light and easy for some, heavy and a real burden for others. It's there, whether you see it or not.

It's simple: Every person you meet has stress, worry, and fear. It's important to remember this as you go into a meeting or address a problem with a buyer. Keep your conversation light and easy. Talk about the buyer, their family, and their business. Keep politics out of the room. If the buyer is having a tough day, you may need to adjust your plan and meet them where they are.

Understanding the temperature in the room is important. No buyer is going to write business if they're in the middle of a stressful event. When you have empathy for people during a tough time, they will appreciate your professionalism and will support you in bigger and better ways.

There is no good reason to continue a meeting when it's obvious there's a problem. Tell the buyer you will reach out in a few days to reschedule and then quietly find the exit. Showing empathy for a tough situation is not only the smart thing, it's the only thing to do. Every person has a bad day including buyers. Being able to recognize when someone is having a bad day is a real skill. When it's obvious the other person is struggling, bow out to serve another day. Yes, it's costly and time-consuming, but it's the smartest thing you can do.

RELIEVE THEIR PAIN

To the novice, the sales professional appears to be a person who shows samples and looks to write orders for commission. In reality, after spending decades with many great professionals, I can tell you the best are all-powerful. They put their customers first and go out of their way to do whatever they can for their customers. They listen extraordinarily well. They help their customers during trying times. They do the core basics very well.

The best reps will make certain their best customers, their top 20%, are taken care of like no one else. Finding and filling needs is essential to help customers succeed. To solve a problem for a customer, they will bring together every company asset necessary to fix it fully and quickly. Besides filling customer needs, taking away some of the pain from your buyer is a real part of growing your status. Know the value of each customer and then go about doing all you can to alleviate the pain as it happens.

TEAM MEMBERS

Selling can be a lonely existence. Sure, you have a sales manager to rely on, but when the most frequent word in your day is No, your world feels vast, and you seem to be the only person in it. But if you look closely, you'll realize how many people are on your team, all helping to smooth out your path. Even for independent sales reps, there is an infrastructure of people working to build and market products that will fit your accounts. As a former sales manager, I appreciate the hard work of the people in the back of the house: production, marketing, accounting, and shipping. Each must do their part to get the products to the account. The longer I worked on the inside, the more I appreciated the efforts of those hired to make the sales team look good.

As a sales rep, many people have your back. They're in place to serve and support your accounts. For a sales organization to work, the team must execute together to help you service your accounts. There is that message that says sales is the lifeblood of the organization and the oxygen that energizes the room on any given day.

But think about how the machine works — think about all the people who make you look like a hero. What if they weren't there? What if they really didn't care about fulfillment or deadlines? Be thankful for their hard work that makes your clock tick in synch. Have patience when you have trouble reaching them; have even more patience when they're calling you with what may seem like endless questions. It's valuable to create relationships with those people who directly affect your success. Send thank you notes, cookies, or other items to show you appreciate their hard work. This will also help you when you have special projects or problems — and you will always have those. Sales is essential for a company's success, but the back office makes the world turn, on time and in full.

VIP RELATIONSHIPS

There are many connections important for your success. Let's look at three internal connections that are vital to operating a smooth, successful territory. They are the relationship with 1) your sales manager, 2) the accounting team, and 3) the shipping department.

Besides being the person responsible for managing a region or division, your sales manager can open doors for you, provide life experience support, and be there long after you've been working together, providing benefits from a career of great experience. Later in your career, your sales manager can help you with leads, recommendations, and inside-track details for new opportunities. He or she is the person you learn from today and gain great benefits from in the future.

The accounting team is essential to your numbers every month because they know when an account may be headed for trouble. Work to find out the birthdays and other important days to recognize. Investing a few dollars into these people is a smart decision.

The same goes for the shipping team. These people work hard, under deadlines, and are rarely recognized. Reward them as often as you can; it will all pay dividends.

Your manager, the accounting team, and the shipping department are working for you, so recognize them often. Thank them whenever possible. Remember, you cannot succeed alone.

RECOGNIZING YOUR COMMUNITY

Your community will grow with your success. It can grow very wide and very deep. Your community consists of clients and prospects, your internal team, your suppliers, and the people they rely on to bring products to the market. In every role, there is an opportunity to grow and build relationships. There is every need to grow the widest community of people possible.

You may be successful today and one of the best in your organization. But times change, companies change, and industries rise and fall. There is a real possibility that one day you will need a helping hand. You may need a connection from a connection.

In the game, Monopoly, the person with the most cash wins. In sales, the person with the deepest network wins, provided you build and strengthen your community.

From the people that repair your vehicle to the people at the hotels where you stay, you need to get to know them all. They're part of your community, your success. Show genuine interest in them. A bunch of small favors adds up to a smoother day with less hassle.

Do things for people in your community whenever possible. Care and concern for your everyday connections will help you build success. Careers are long, so gaining support along the way can be priceless. Learn more and more about the people in your community. When they're on your side, climbing the success ladder takes less energy and time.

When it really matters

When I was a buyer, I had suppliers, and then I had suppliers I trusted in a pinch. They made a great deal of extra money because I knew I could count on them. When a buyer must have something in their hands on a specific day, and there's no plan B, they will only call their most trusted people to get it done. Your goal should be to be that person.

Once you have earned this level of trust, you have to carry the ball all the way when special orders come to you. No matter the day or situation, be certain that everyone on your team understands the urgency. In these situations, cost is generally secondary. Yes, you still want to know any special charges, including shipping, and communicate them to the buyer. But with the most critical orders, the assurance of receiving the product on time, is the goal.

Becoming the trusted supplier holds great sway. When a buyer places a critical order in your hands, they are trusting you. It's essential to make sure your team is in the loop. It's one thing to earn this level of trust, and another to maintain it. In my experience, it's impossible for a rep to fail when they enable their accounts to win.

Word of mouth

As a consumer, what do you do when you consider a significant purchase? You look for every meaningful review, as well as talk to people about their experience with the product or service. Before the internet, people asked others about their experiences; in sales, the path is the same. When a buyer wants to know about a brand or product, they'll call buyers they trust for their opinion. Getting a 5-star review from a buyer is the best way to improve your reach.

Word-of-mouth support is powerful and the most trusted way to earn face time with a buyer. Know that when you do reach out for a buyer's recommendation, it's a big favor. So you must acknowledge the support and show gratitude. Getting a solid recommendation from another buyer is better than advertising. When you reach out to ask for help, do it with caution, do it sparingly, and follow up. And be extraordinary in your service execution with the new account: Buyers talk with each other.

MAKE THE TIME, ENJOY THE PEOPLE

Days fly by. Months and years fall off the calendar. Sales is just like time: it never stands still. There are goals to reach, problems to solve, and buyers to meet. There never seems to be a time out, a time to just drink it all in, and revel in the world.

My time is behind me. I no longer have the ability to appreciate the world and people around me. You, on the other hand, are in the game, moving Heaven and Earth for that next order. Every day is meant to be busy. When it's not, your manager expects you to add cold calls to the menu.

My suggestion: stop where you are every so often and spend time with your favorite industry people. Even if it's just an extra 30 minutes, have a meaningful conversation, asking about how the person is doing. As you plan out your week and month, look for those spots where you can step off the tracks to see the people on your favorites list. It will brighten their day and make you feel like a lottery winner. One day, your career will be behind you. A few minutes in the day can mean a lot to others and in time and priceless to you. You will be glad you did.

Selling Stew: Grand Lessons without the Theme

The following lessons did not fit into one of the standard categories in this book, but they are valuable nonetheless. These lessons can provide valuable knowledge and insight. Recognizing that many sales professionals have the same anxieties and concerns helps make us all feel a bit more human. As you dig into this section, you will find valuable content you can use — it just didn't fit under a specific chapter title. Enjoy these odd points of value. Although they may not be a part of your every week, they will come across your desk at some point.

THE BUSINESS BEYOND THE SALE

As I matured in my job, I looked to spend time with the smart people within my industry. It became almost an obsession as being curious about successful execution became my daily habit. Over my career, I have worked with a lot of sales professionals. Many of them were great at presentations, others excelled in all areas of their business. I searched for the smart people because this was the group that hit my radar. As a young buyer, I wanted to hang out with the older, confident professionals, understanding how they achieved success.

As you grow in this job, it's no longer a nice thing to explore the work beyond your job description, it's a must-do. As a sales pro, you touch many people in several departments. From manufacturing, to supply chain management, accounting, warehousing, and marketing, you are exposed to an entire business operation.

You also most likely work with sales management several days a week. These days, opportunities come in the blink of an eye. If you have a working knowledge of the business beyond your role, you will be prepared when your number is called. Even if you remain in sales, understanding the entire business framework will make you the go-to professional for bigger and better territories.

THAT YES MAY TAKE SOME TIME

Have you noticed that many people give up too soon? It seems that just as they pick up some momentum, they decide to pack it in. They lose hope, believing their attempt would result only in wasted time and effort. They give up before they have a shot at winning.

In sales, there can be no walking away. There are limited territories, each of limited size. The sales professional has open accounts, inactive accounts, and prospects. Their success depends on their drive and patience. Some orders come easily, others take time, maybe a great deal of time.

As a buyer, spending time with a sales rep meant I had some interest in their product lineup. It was the rep's job to convince me that their product line would work for my customers. If there was a good fit and I got the deal I wanted, I moved forward. But if the rep thought I was an easy mark, they were about to be disappointed. Think about the things you wanted in your career. How many interviews did you have to endure? How much patience did you have to muster?

In sales, it comes down to you figuring out exactly how to tap into the needs of each account. Never give up on your accounts. Certainly, never give up on your buyers. Know that buyers get busy. They have multiple priorities, with several constituencies, vying for their time. You never really know why you are on the back burner, so you need to always push forward, assuming one day the lights will turn green.

WHAT KEEPS YOU UP

Every one of us has worry, stress, and doubt. There are any number of items that can keep our eyes wide open at night. Will you receive that large order, open the new account or solve the mystery of a key account going away? Will you hit the monthly numbers, achieve the bonus and build momentum toward a successful year-end? The reasons to toss and turn are seemingly endless. If tossing and turning brings you no closer to your goals, why would you allow everyday work challenges to rob you of sleep?

Many years ago I took away a great lesson from a sales conference: Control your controllables. Concern yourself with those issues you can change. Thinking you can change anything above your paygrade is unrealistic. Worry becomes stress and prevents successful execution.

Life is about being prepared, as ready as you can be to manage the ups and downs of your role. When you pitch to an account, bringing all you can, you can rest easy, knowing you did your best. You don't know exactly how the buyer feels or what competitors have to present. No sleepless night ever made a sale happen or created a large order. Do all you can in the waking hours, the time you are paid to plan, prepare, and execute. Control the controllables and keep the stress out of the bedroom.

QUESTIONS

There were many times I would second-guess myself as to why I booked an appointment with a particular supplier. I did not believe in the product or even the sales rep. In fact, I would get angry with myself. I never wanted to waste time going down a path I had little interest in exploring. When I questioned myself, this is what I asked:

- What does this rep want to show me?

- What is the quantity they might expect me to purchase?

- Will they appreciate that sales are down and inventory is high?

- Will they present a plan to help us sell their product? About marketing and presentation?
- Might they have off-price goods I can buy to improve the margins?
- Will this meeting be a total waste of time?

As a sales pro, you should be constantly thinking about time. Realize it can be a sacrifice for a buyer to provide time to meet, especially face-to-face. Respect the time your buyer provides. Be prepared, ready with samples and your story. Deliver a tight, succinct message in the time provided. When you provide the essential details up front, move through your presentation, answer all questions, and leave time for a summary, you're showing respect for the buyer's time. You never need to rush, but you do need to use your time wisely to achieve your mission.

SELLING AS A COMPANY REP

Sales is truly a wonderful career. Being a company employee, working within a system, is one way to build a career. Working for a solid organization with established accounts and a meaningful product line will help establish your name and reputation in your industry.

In the end, however, it's all about you, the rep. Do accounts like and trust you? Will the important buyers give you a fair shot? This path for young people is an especially rewarding direction. Many times, organizations provide a small salary and benefits. Some even provide a vehicle. A new rep can gain a great education serving in a company role. Gaining experience building presentation skills while learning to manage a territory is priceless. Jumping in with an established organization can provide solid footing and important time to build success.

The benefits of becoming a company sales rep include:
- A consistent salary or draw.
- Health insurance benefits.

- Support with expenses.
- A retirement program.
- Samples provided at no charge.
- A team able and ready to support your efforts.

Working for one organization is a proven route for young men and women who want to establish a strong footing in sales. It can also be a solid landing spot for older, mature professionals with an established reputation. These reps no longer want the pressure of commission-only programs. Deciding between becoming a company or an independent sales rep comes down to a personal decision. It depends on the family situation, financial needs, and other individual factors. Long-term company reps like the comfort and support of the organization. It comes down to personal comfort and individual need.

Selling as an independent rep

Being an independent sales rep is ideal for those with great confidence and willingness to walk the riskier side of the road. Being an independent rep means you may have a sales manager for each supplier, but you are mostly on your own. You decide what, when, and how to present. There are no micromanagers in your world. You build your own calendar and take days off when you want. The pay is all commission-based. There may be bonuses for achieving certain benchmarks, but there is no salary, health plan or retirement program to grow over time.

There can be any number of rules for independent sales professionals within your industry. Many companies limit the number of suppliers you can represent. If an industry has a shortage of good reps, the gloves come off and the options become wider and wider. Know that for every supplier you represent, you will have:

- A sales manager.
- A credit manager.
- A customer service manager.
- A vice president of sales.

As long as you can manage the number of people within your community, you can succeed on a grand scale. Unlike most company sales roles, there really is no limit to the money an independent rep can earn.

A big downside, however, is the expenses. All expenses, including travel, hotel, food, and so on will all come out of your pocket. You are also responsible for reporting and paying your own taxes; the companies do not withhold taxes for you.

For many successful sales professionals, the independent route is one taken after years spent working for a single organization. These reps have put together a strong cash reserve and are willing to work without a company safety net. They have a stellar reputation with accounts and want the freedom of creating their own calendar. They understand the world they serve and move forward with eyes wide open.

The vast majority of independent reps I've worked with stay independent. They like the income, the freedom, and the ability to manage their own world. Based on your comfort, needs, and your family's needs, you can work for a company or work for yourself. In the end, the daily execution is the same. It comes down to how you want to manage your career and your life.

TRIAL BALLOONS

During my years in the buyer's seat, I witnessed pitch after pitch after pitch. As my career advanced, I realized that reps, on most occasions, would swing for the fences, trying to convince me to buy big and grab more inventory on the front end of the product cycle. Some suggested numbers so large, no buyer in their right mind would have signed off. They had the belief that even if the number was too large, the strength of the organization would absorb any upfront excess. These attempts never worked.

I witnessed it several times before, being a victim early in my experience as a buyer. After a number of these, I pushed to the opposite extreme: I would begin with a minimum purchase and slowly work up to numbers that made sense to all of my locations, based on sell-through momentum.

My suggestion to them (and now to you) is unless you are

totally confident in your request, the size of the opportunity, and your brand's support, a trial balloon can be the answer. A trial balloon is a small delivery to top locations, building out the presentation, marketing, and product training. If the buyer sees the product turning well, you and your buyer then build out a series of purchase orders to meet the needs of each location.

Trial balloons take time, which means sales managers do not like them. They dislike the order size and lack of faith. But they're smart strategies for building confidence with your buyer.

If you're right, a new, larger order with backups will flow quickly. As you gain these small wins, you're also building integrity with your buyer. We know that the name on your business card may change, but most accounts will remain intact. You must always protect your relationship with your buyers because they'll stay the same if you stay within your industry.

One other suggestion: When you do go for the home run, it's essential to build a specific volume model per location. Every organization has A, B, and C locations. No organization will buy the same number of widgets across the board. Work to understand the total business and develop models that make sense for each individual location.

THE GRAY MARKET

Suppliers in every industry develop and market products from time to time that get very hot. In that moment, every account wants the product in full while the rep can never find enough. Most suppliers place these hot products on allocation, hopefully ensuring existing accounts acquire at least some of what they want.

At the same time, most accounts want as much as they can receive. They'll sometimes stop at nothing to pull in as much inventory as they can get their hands on. Suppliers generally provide allocation based on the previous success of each territory. Since most products have bar codes and/or serial numbers, products can be tracked.

In this situation, it's important to know the internal rules; you don't want to lose your job over what you think is a bit of extra commission. Going above your allocation and planting extra inventory with friendly buyers is not the thing to do. Stick with the rules of your organization, or you'll risk creating havoc all around.

Ship all of the hot products possible from your allocation, but don't go beyond the rules, regardless of the account. Accounts may even offer a small premium to acquire more of the hot item, but you'll create bigger problems for yourself.

Stay away from the gray market. I have seen it burn too many people and organizations. Sales reps lose jobs and accounts lose relationships with key brands. As a rep, deliver all you can within the rules and be happy with the success in the moment. More will follow.

Selling closeouts

All products have a life cycle. Some products seem never to work, even from the outset. At some point, most suppliers will have a closeout offer, in order to sell off the poor movers. They have too much inventory or stuff that no one wants to buy at the standard wholesale.

In addition, because products have life cycles, some once-popular products live on shelves a bit too long. At some point, the supplier will put together an off-price list. If small in number, it becomes all about getting to that list first, picking the best products, and shipping everything the buyers can use. Off-price products generally start at 20 – 25% off. The commissions, however, shrink by as much as half, so many sales reps avoid closeouts. They don't like making a sale for less than top commission.

So here's a secret most sales reps ignore: If your primary focus is your customer, then you may want to be in the closeout business. You can become a hero at both ends. You can reduce inventory for your organization while providing your buyers a way to enhance both sales and margin. Your buyers are happy while your sales manager is excited because you're reducing poor inventory.

Smart buyers will cost average some of their purchases, especially their off-price purchases. Mixing in low-priced products will allow buyers to grow margins while also increasing sales. If you decide to handle closeouts, don't worry about the loss of commission. If you work with your best accounts, you're building a strong bond with buyers who will remember the opportunities. Providing a continuous string of real benefits for your top accounts will enable you to grow a very strong territory.

FIRING A CUSTOMER

Every account should matter. From the relationships you build to the orders you write, at some level all accounts matter. Look at every account in your territory as a long-term, appreciating asset. You'll create a sense of urgency and provide the service you would expect if the roles were reversed. Certainly from the start, you have the highest hopes for every account you open and every prospect. However, issues get in the way of your best intentions. Things like bad credit, slow pay, new leadership, or even a new buyer coming in with a new program that excludes you.

You may try to do all you can to save an account, there are other voices in the room that matter. Your sales manager, credit manager, and even VP of sales may have something to say about an account and its ability to remain open.

The one roadblock that can end a relationship is the issue of credit. Not paying invoices on time or leaving several open will force suppliers to stop selling to an account. Because you have a limited number of potential accounts, every one should have value. But if the situation becomes sour, there is no reason to continue a dialogue with the buyer. The organization may ask you to help collect past-due invoices, but the chance to write orders again will probably not be an option.

In essence, you're firing the customer. So long before you get to the point of termination, look at the credit reports every other week. When there are signs of trouble, have a meeting with the buyer; credit issues should be discussed face-to-face. You need to learn the facts, help your organization, and see if you can help the account. Bad credit is a problem that will be around as long as people do business. The best time to put out the fire is when you see the smoke. Help your organization and your buyers by keeping an eye on things that can end relationships.

BUYERS: A UNIQUE VARIETY PACK

Although I have not written a purchase order since 2010, an old industry friend recently gave me a 10-second report card of what salespeople thought of my attitude as a buyer. He said I was "tough, but fair." This is a man I like very much and deeply respect. His words at this time in my life stung a bit. I have spent a few decades trying to lose the word "tough" from my industry resume. Although it hurt when I heard it several weeks ago, it wouldn't have bothered me throughout most of my years on the job. I probably would have reveled in that phrase. Buyers are as different as their fingerprints. In my case, I worked with blinders. I cared about the organization and getting the best deal at that moment. Nothing else mattered. It was about who paid my salary and the mission that day. That was where I spent my loyalty.

As a sales rep, you also have a mission. You're looking to write orders and build long-term positive relationships with buyers and the accounts they serve. Sales reps must come at the job with sensitivity and nuance. Buyers are more bull in the china shop mode.

Over your career, you will meet a great variety of buyers. Some are nice and a bit quiet. Others will attack you the minute you touch your samples and never relent. You'll learn to develop a different playbook for each account. It's important to write notes for every meeting with your buyers. You'll see ways to play off their personalities in order to achieve your mission.

Buyers will test you. Some may be yellers, others will push and push until they get what they want, or you're forced to bring in reinforcements in the form of sales management.

Each buyer comes with a mission. You may have the product, but they hold the purchase order. Although a dogfight may ensue, the end game is about positioning products, making money for both sides, and creating a mutually successful business. How you arrive is a very different matter. Never be intimidated. Remain focused on the mission, your presentation, and where you want to be at the end.

Your buyer wants to buy, otherwise, they would not be investing time and energy. If you feel disrespected, halt the proceedings, reset the ground rules, and see what happens next. If you continue to feel out of sorts, you may need to hand this account over to your manager for a different plan.

Attitude

> "Success is the sum of small efforts, repeated day in and day out."
>
> Robert Collier.

You have a choice every morning: you can decide what face you'll wear. You get to choose how to approach the day. Beginning with a great attitude is your best choice. When you develop a positive, can-do attitude, you will influence more people. Professionals like to hang around positive people. Buyers want to be with people who like people. On the other hand, buyers are not fans of people who complain or talk about why they failed to hit last month's numbers. Work constantly on your attitude, otherwise it's easy to fall back and become complacent. A great attitude takes constant work and reminding as each day throws several curves your way. Look to be the best part of your customers' day.

WIDEN, THEN STRETCH YOUR VISION

As you grow both experience and success in your territory and organization, it becomes easy to feel like an expert. It's like the third baseman in baseball. He is the expert in the hot corner and knows the position exceedingly well, but spends no time in other parts of the field, understanding the situation from the other positions. Unlike that third baseman, you can't afford to take a narrow view, or worse, to become the great expert in that one area.

It's important to widen your view and be curious about your

entire organization. How it is doing overall, what are the possibilities as well as its shortcomings? It's also important to dig deeper into the accounts you serve. As you learn more, you may discover opportunities you might not connect to without a deep dive into the other suppliers, their marketing, and operations. As you learn more about your customers, opportunities will become apparent. The more you know, the better your ability to present ideas and programs for your accounts, especially the top 20%. They do more business and may be open to your ideas for trials of new products. Never just ask for the order, but present a success plan that results in more sales and profits for your buyer.

Widen your view of each account. Get to understand their business beyond the dealings you share. Search for cracks in relationships and opportunities not visible without digging. Learn all you can about your competitors. The more you know, the more weaknesses you will uncover, discovering the cracks and holes you should be able to fill. The way to the top begins with extra effort and results from the due diligence most others are not willing to put in.

Information is the next great currency. Know more to earn more. The more influencers you know, the more information you will learn. Stretch your efforts to build your future. Begin to help more people. Begin to search for those cracks lying just under the surface.

NEVER BELIEVE IN NEVER

The longer you remain in any industry, the more you will hear crazy notions from just about every direction. For years, sales reps, their managers, and brand leaders told me over and over, that certain things were simply never going to happen. They were never going to add certain colors, add styles, or develop a certain brand extension or product model. None of this was going to take place.

But I would chat with other buyers over and over again about why the never-going-to-happen projects should happen. Buyers develop very good instincts. They watch the numbers, visit their organization's locations, talk to the sales team, and know what should come next. Buyers are a very good source of what should happen.

A supplier might say never, but leaders change and numbers sag. What was simply not doable yesterday may be up for discussion next quarter. Organizations need growth; they must add sales and profit or they fade away. New is the magic word. New products, styles, colors, and even categories are the means for growth.

Suppliers also want more and more shelf space. I have never heard a salesperson ask to shrink their product footprint, especially with key accounts. Try not to develop your list of favorite items to sell, because you may push aside a better-selling product. Talk with your manager about the expectations from their side and work with that list.

Goals never go down. New managers and leaders demand change and growth. They'll never accept the status quo. It's important to to never fall into the never going to happen conversation. No matter what you hear in meetings or in everyday conversation about those things, people, circumstances, and missed budgets can put just about anything on the table. When you hear the Never-word when new product ideas are batted about, leave those conversations in the room.

Don't get into conversations with buyers about future ideas or products. Your mission is to sell your current catalog and leave the wish list ideas to the product development team.

NEVER ASSUME

Why do salespeople assume that buyers know exactly what they sell? For years, I was frustrated by sales reps who thought I knew the full scope of their product catalog. Why would I? How could I when I was juggling so many balls in the air? It was their job to school me on the product lines and reasons I may have an interest. Since I was buying for large organizations, many reps also assumed I would naturally be writing a large order after a presentation.

This lesson is a valuable one: Never assume a sale. You have to earn it. Although your buyer is also preparing for the meeting, you're the expert. It's important to provide the essential information as to why your buyer should invest in your products.

Understand how your product can fit into the business for every buyer. Tell them what your organization is about and where they fit in the specific markets they play in. Build stories about your brand, products, and territory. People want to hear about successes and how your products will make their business better. Don't cut to the end or talk only about your top items. If your buyer doesn't want to hear about the full menu, they'll cut you off. Don't assume you know what your buyer wants to hear. And never assume you will walk out of the room with an order just because you did solid prep work.

DO THE WORK, THEN REPEAT AND REPEAT

At its core, sales is often about rejection. But it's a matter of finding the energy to push forward in anticipation of the next Yes. Over several weeks, you may acquire a few wins. And there will be times when booking appointments seems nearly impossible. Rejection stings no doubt, but the wins help to soften the scars. Over time, there will be extraordinary wins. These wins come with commissions. However, they will not come with applause or even a simple pat on the back. Sales is the ultimate self-starter enterprise. You have to want to do the work, create the accounts, and tell your story.

The role has tough days, and it has amazing days. So it's important to balance your emotions as your system moves from rejection to rejection to major order. Some days, the job doesn't seem to make much sense. You make one presentation and get rejected out of hand while the one stop you make just to check in provides you with the largest order of the week.

Consistency is a winning piece of the success formula. Serve your buyers well. They will be the reasons you keep doing what you do. A successful career is built one day at a time. Don't allow the down times to alter your story or your plan.

GRATITUDE

I have known and worked with thousands of sales professionals. Many have sold millions of dollars in products, earning millions over their career. There were other reps who never achieved those results. In fact, several had difficulty meeting their monthly expenses. Although the two examples are very different life situations, their view of the profession was just about equal: they loved what they did!

They loved the road, interactions with buyers, training, trips, opportunities, and their status in the industry. These people also loved the freedom. They were never going to be desk jockeys, dialing for dollars, or other efforts that would eventually drown their enthusiasm.

Successful reps, those who jump out of bed, excited for their first sales call, have genuine gratitude. They love the work, the challenge, and the relationships. These things are the fuel for their tank. This is a group of people truly grateful for their work. Not every day is a winning day, but each one offers them the opportunity to build success. Many of the older reps especially cherish the relationships developed over the years. They keep the reps motivated and eager to strike out on yet another day. Just as in sports where each new game begins with no score, each new day brings an open, clean slate to the sale rep. It is their mission to post numbers.

No matter where the work takes you, be grateful for every role. Be grateful for the climb, rejections, and education each day can bring. Money gets spent quickly, but relationships can be nurtured for a lifetime.

This is an important lesson: Selling is a complex profession with landmines all about. It's important to present a great attitude and share a story complete with personal knowledge. Sales is a unique, open-ended opportunity. No matter the trials and potholes, appreciate your freedom to grow, earn, and create an amazing life.

Success

"Never confuse activity with results."
Lou Gerstner.

Most of us have our own definition of success. Although there is more than one, success comes from dreams, and everyone has the chance to dream. As you think about what it means to you, add your goals into the mix. Achieving goals certainly means you are obtaining success. As a sales pro, you will also always have company goals to achieve. Take them seriously, doing all you can to beat expectations. At the same time, never allow your company goals to replace your professional goals. Think about creating goals for the next 36 months, one year at a time. Add in personal goals and you have created a clear path for a successful life.

BE THE EVER-CONSUMING LEARNER

Being on the road is one of the hallmarks of a career in sales. The road warrior is that person moving from place to place in search of customers, orders, and an ever-growing territory. Being on the road provides the opportunity to become a great listener and learner.

From the many great business podcasts to books on tape, there is quality content far beyond music and sports talk available anytime you hit the road. In 2023, there are unlimited reasons — and ways — to continue listening and learning. Listening in the vehicle between appointments is simply an investment in your future. Curiosity is a great gift. Digging into new and different subjects can keep you excited and invested in your profession.

The day you left school was only a break in your education, not the conclusion. Since every industry changes, you need to develop a program of continuous learning, as you travel every month. Ask your sales manager what they might recommend in the way of continuous learning programs. Between audiobooks, podcasts, and YouTube, there is a never-ending curriculum of valuable content.

In addition to the road content, think about conferences, webinars, and other ways to connect with the upcoming movers and shakers. Sales and its accompanying education can be rewarding. Here you can create your own personal masterclass. It will take the latest information to help manage the challenges you'll encounter. Remain curious and continue searching for new content.

SEARCHING FOR THE VITAL SKILLS AND VALUES

No matter the organization, every person wants to know the important next skills that will move them forward. What will success look like in three years? Five years? What is their optimum path? There is no doubt that being a buyer helped me succeed when I joined the other side. During my buying years, I wanted several times to get in a sales rep's face and tell them exactly how to service and manage my accounts.

I was never concerned about their commission numbers or what my purchase order might do for them. But I did want to help my reps understand how to make things better between us. I never took the time to lay these thoughts out, so I'm including them here. I believe they're essential in creating a great service environment:

- Spend time living in the buyer's shoes.

- Know the buyer has many suppliers and probably too much inventory.

- Their decisions are made for the benefit of the business.

- Show empathy for each and every account.
- Become an extraordinary communicator.
- Present your entire lineup, unless told otherwise, as it will create brand extensions.
- Dig into customer concerns, without delay or drama.
- Create the same sense of urgency in addressing customer issues as when shipping orders.

Based on your industry and customer segment, you may have additional items to develop. The list above can bring respect, access, and success your way. Continue to hone your skills as you search for other items that will bring you closer to your customer.

LOVE THE GAME

Many people find their way into selling. They heard it was a great place to make money, so they jumped in with both feet. It could be real estate, consumer goods, or maybe pharmaceuticals. They believed the path would lead to a world with significant income and an overall grand life. For a variety of reasons, their path led into a ditch. Selling was just not their deal.

Others, you included, had a thirst for sales. You knew successful salespeople and knew it was what you wanted to do. It was to be more than a job, it became your mission. The mission to build a successful career with a territory. Salespeople with a mission do their work and go forth in both good times and bad times. If they lose a role with one company, they quickly look to get back on the horse repping for the next one. These men and women who continue to push forward are the real professionals.

They go in with a plan to get things done. They don't make excuses, no matter the situation. Each day they have a plan and a series of benchmarks to achieve. They enjoy the freedom and the work they get to do each day. They love their customers and know that if they take care of them, their income will grow. They love the action of face-to-face meetings. The game is what counts, the commission is the final score. Because they love it, they rarely get down, no matter the local circumstances or the economy. They truly love to sell and consider any other work a chore that's meant for other people.

TRUST, THE OTHER MAJOR SUCCESS TRAIT

In another section of this book I detailed that being liked is a top priority for anyone who wants to succeed in selling. Being liked allows access, which means you can get a meeting. Selling is more than just a standard-length game. For a salesperson to play and win over the long term, the buyer must trust them.

Being trusted is the other major priority. Would you do business with an electrician you didn't trust or buy a car from someone you did not trust? People do business with people they trust.

Trust is the glue that can create a long-term relationship. It takes a long time to earn and no time to lose. Being liked is the gateway and being trusted gets you a seat at the table. Earn trust for the long term and you become a partner. You can never take it for granted. Trust is about always telling the truth, no matter the short-term costs. It is about never compromising your values. To do business with one buyer or account for a long time, total honesty must be part of your tool kit.

YET ANOTHER IMPORTANT SUCCESS TRAIT

Follow up! Earn a reputation as a sales rep who is amazing at following up with buyers and accounts. Buyers look for reps who pay attention beyond receiving the order. They'll go out of their way to do more business with the professional who completes the circle, manages with great follow-up, and handles their problems. Becoming this person will enable you to supersize your reputation and career. The other tangible benefit of excelling in follow-up is the opportunity to build your account base. Buyers will be happy to recommend you to other buyers.

INVEST IN YOUR BUSINESS

Building a career in sales means making both commitments and investments in your success. Investing in the proper vehicle for the work you do is one of your most important decisions. Many sales reps I know have diesel-powered vehicles because they historically enjoy many more years on the road than gasoline-powered cars.

Invest in sales contests for your buyers and their sales people. Creating sales contests will help promote your brand, sell products, and and excite the people who move the goods. Also, offer recognition awards to thank buyers for their support. Few things are more valuable than being recognized. Make time on your calendar to get lunch with buyers. In addition to showing your gratitude, spending time with them can bring you valuable information about the territory and other suppliers. Spending time with people in your territory will enhance friendships and help to build valuable business relationships.

INVEST IN YOURSELF

There is no better long-term investment than investing in yourself. A personal development plan is a smart way to grow your skills and income over your career. Here are a few ideas of what to include in a plan.

- Be a reader. Build a library that includes great business books as well as biographies about people you admire.
- Attend webinars in your industry.
- Attend industry conferences.
- Join a speaking club, like Toastmasters International.
- Get a mentor or a coach.
- Review your plan every two years to determine any changes you want to make.

Building a better you is essential. In good times and bad, invest in finding information and gaining new skills for your business. Improvement matters. As the grey hairs increase and competition gets younger, your knowledge and desire to keep learning will keep you at the top of your world. Never stop learning or investing in yourself.

ACCESS

When you have options in life: when you gain access to the most critical people in your community, you have an open door most can only dream about.

As young people, we search for the good company, the job that gets the wheels to turn. Before then, we can't even get a conversation started. As a rep, we want the bigger, better territory, but lack the experience to be considered. As an experienced sales professional, we have the experience, but not the skills to move into sales management. Gaining access to the skills, the situations, and the right people is the goal. These are the situations to create your best path.

The other secret is to remain persistent. To keep asking and not deviate from the things you want. If everyone who was ever turned down a first time, went away, never to ask again, no one would ever succeed. Access is getting the "A" ticket to all you want to achieve in your career.

Summary
Selling in the Real World

"Value the relationship more than making the quota."
Jeffrey Gitomer.

Being on the other side of the buyer's desk, believing you must write an order at that moment is a daunting feeling. Certainly, it exists for a number of salespeople. There are varying degrees of week-to-week demands on both the supplier and their sales team.

The larger the brand, the less stress at that desk. With challenger brands, those suppliers looking for a leg up always feel pressure for a good outcome with every encounter. The seller is looking for the opportunity for the "yes."

The great challenge to provide strong ideas happens with the salesperson. They're the ones who will create something from nothing. The best sales reps make a good career better, through caring, creating, and servicing their clients. Follow-up is the last piece of that success pie.

There are a few essential takeaways to reinforce from this side of the desk. It seems that on the buyer's side, homework and preparation are the necessities for winning. On the sales side, the values include all of the above, plus many more. The sales pro must prepare for any meeting with a customer or prospect. They must know the sales numbers, the open orders, and the history of the account. They must be likable just to get in the room. They must be trustworthy to build a relationship with the buyers. And they must be persistent; many orders do not arrive until the third or fourth attempt. Finally, there's follow-up: it's rarer than you can imagine, but it can turn an average sales career into a grand one.

One Final Story

AN INTENSE SENSE OF URGENCY

This is a unique story. The sales executive in this story is the most intense professional I have ever known. He was willing to do anything to gain a face to face meeting with a buyer.

I have worked with many sales professionals. Some moved quickly, others moved at their own pace. There was one who moved at a different pace from all the rest. He was the Vice President of Sales for an organization, based in Western Canada. When given the opportunity to meet with a key buyer he would jump on a plane, at a moment's notice, just to get face-to-face with his intended prospect for as little as 30 minutes.

I found it to be unbelievable when I was first involved with his brand, but he did it over and over again with multiple buyers. If a buyer gave him access, he did everything to make it work. He had a sense of urgency far different than any sales professional I've ever known. He understood the value of a meeting. He certainly understood the value of working with key buyers.

Once given the appointment, even if it was the following day, this pro scheduled the flight, flew to the meeting, and made things happen. His product? He represented a line of sunglasses with wholesale prices ranging from $35 to $55. This relationship goes back 30-plus years. I have since forgotten this person's name but his sheer sense of urgency was unlike anything I had ever experienced before or since."

Thoughts at Halftime

"Caring about the happiness of others, we find our own."

Plato

Here we are at halftime, taking the reader from the sales side of the desk to the buyer's chair. We are now smack in the middle — halftime, as it were. We're transitioning from offense to defense: moving you to where the decisions are made that most impact the future of an organization. Buying is the nucleus of many organizations. Get it right and watch sales and profits soar. Make too many mistakes, the margin loss will certainly cost a great deal.

The ideas below are thoughts for you to chew on. During halftime, they provide a positive distraction. They might be meaningful for you and prove to be of value. The ideas below might be for buyers, but they can also engage sellers. And they might just apply to all.

Thoughts that can make a difference:

- Differentiate or die.
- Invest your time towards major results.
- Ask all of your questions before you end the meeting.
- Get all of your questions answered.
- Understand the mindset of the billboard: message received in 3-5 seconds.
- The best-laid plans often go sideways.
- Never stop hustling.
- Disruption is the new way.
- All in your community should believe in the purchase.
- In tough times, rely on your best relationships for support information and business.

- Be grateful, always.
- Send hand-written thank you notes in record numbers.
- Adapt, adapt, adapt.
- Information is the new currency.
- What are your best practices?
- Never assume.
- Take time always to review your results. The homework matters.
- Develop great basics. Execute your great basics daily.
- Practice with pennies, not $100 bills.
- Everyone has access to information. You must go beyond to become a trusted advisor.
- Never stop asking for what you want. Continue to negotiate.
- Spite is not a strategy.
- What are you willing to change or discard in order to improve?
- Explain to the other side why you made that decision.
- Get out of bed each day to do something extraordinary.
- What is your end game?
- It's more than about ideas, it's about execution.
- Be willing to make mistakes.
- Fake confidence until you can own the room.
- Devote your career to becoming a great listener.
- Be humble. Be always willing to ask for feedback.
- Great energy encourages action.
- I have never run low on suppliers. I have never had too many customers.
- There is a cost to every activity.
- Build a plan, work that plan.
- Whatever you create, there has to be a profit attached.
- Everyone loves the shiny, new object.
- Think wider.
- What are your 5 musts as a buyer?
- What are your 5 musts as a seller?
- Sweat the details.
- No manager or leader likes surprises.
- What rules will you break or recreate?
- What new roads will you construct?

- What items should come off of your calendar forever?
- What new items should be a part of your calendar going forward?
- Make owning the thing fun!
- Get smarter, get better, and never stop learning.
- How is social media working for you?
- What is your process and strategy?
- Look for cracks. Every business has opportunities. Every business has cracks.

It's good to know there is more than one way to win. Much of the effort to get to that place is about trial and error, just as with most of life. One of the important lessons I learned years ago was to become an intense sponge. As I ascended into larger roles, I had the opportunity to work with very smart people. They not only provided sensational pointers on discovering new ways forward, they also showed me how incredible people think and build winning strategies. Being a sponge is an essential part of any plan to improve.

As we exit the section on selling, moving into the buying space, think about how you might use this halftime content. They may provide the beginnings of a new plan and direction. To grow, win, and survive at a high level means updating your plan regularly. Tweak it for growth and improvement. Searching to find the better road ahead makes you a visionary. But if you're not getting better, you're getting worse. Just like the pilot for your next flight, develop a flight plan to fit your career aspirations. Never stop improving. It's the oxygen that feeds your career. Always think a few steps ahead and keep moving to where the puck is going.

Lessons to grow your knowledge, grow your skills, build your career

Section Titles

- Leadership
- Preparation
- Planning
- Execution
- Organization
- Management
- Relationships
- Communications
- Buyer's Stew
- Marketing
- Attitude
- Success

To my mind, buying is the best way to spend eight, ten, twelve hours of any workday. Imagine being handed a role, a title, and a checkbook. You get to look at the products you want, the products you believe will work. You go to special events, shows, and locations that are just a bit beyond spectacular, all the while being treated royally. So, when does the work begin?

It is not hard to see why, after thirty years and several stops along the journey, I was shattered when my buying position was eliminated. The Great Recession hit hard and lasted for several years, taking down people and businesses. In the end, I had three decades of joy, amazing friendships, and success, all while being treated better than any person deserved. Looking back on those years, they were better than great. No doubt, I wished I would have stopped to enjoy and to experience each day a bit more.

Now that my tour has ended, let's look at buying as a position, an integral part of an organization. The buyer is a leader and a member of the management team. Although they have their head down reviewing numbers, history, products, and programs much of the time, a buyer works to further the organization in every way. As a manager, a buyer feels ownership and works to improve their organization and team. They realize the decisions they make have a direct impact on their business. The buyer sits at the core of the entire effort, no matter who is pushing the ball forward in the moment.

Every buyer has a level of fear, but good buyers push through it. They understand their role and they do it well. They create a lot of tries and trials, searching for that next great head-turner that will increase foot traffic and sales. The good buyer quickly recognizes buying mistakes. They take corrective action to move poor products, freeing up cash to engage the next decision.

Buyers make mistakes. The experienced ones will minimize them, trying never to expose their organization to a bloated risk. Certainly, buyers miss things, make some silly decisions, or forget to execute on a special buy. It all comes with the territory. Buyers are busy. They work hard to manage their time to maximize results daily for the enterprise.

This portion of the book has 12 sections digging into the role of the buyer. Each category has several lessons created to inform, support, and help the reader discover new skills, uncover a few tricks, and several real strategies, all with the expectation to achieve greater results. There are thirty years of experience supporting each lesson.

Buying is a grand opportunity to marry data with daily hard knocks experience. It's important a buyer believes in more than the spreadsheet filled with historical detail. The buyer should believe in their intuition. The data can provide a great deal of information, it's important however, for the buyer to gain the instinct as to when a buy is a smart decision.

Consumer-centric organizations go out of business due many times to owning too much inventory. The buyer role, therefore, encompasses so much more than picking and choosing products. They have a long litany of tasks to do to help the organization achieve desired results. This book will hopefully provide ideas that will serve you well today and over the course of your time as a buyer.

Leadership

"When everything seems to be going against you, remember that the airplane takes off against the wind, not with it."

Henry Ford

As a buyer, you head up a critical part of the organization. Certainly, you may have a small group of people in your department, but leadership in this context goes beyond directing people. It means being in control of your department. Developing successful programs with suppliers, while communicating your message to your team presents unique opportunities. As buyers succeed, they no doubt learn to take charge and negotiate more of what they want for their organization. Leadership plays an important part in the role of a buyer. The more responsibility you get, the more leadership will be expected of you. You will set an important example to many within your organization.

OWN THE ROOM

As the buyer, you're in charge of the process, it therefore should be your decision where a presentation should take place. When you control the space, you hold court on your terms, and you control the atmosphere. If you don't like how things are progressing, you can end the session.

As I gained experience, I insisted that my meetings be held in my office or our conference room. Suppliers generally have a different plan. Their goal is to meet where they control the space. During my career, salespeople worked to move me to their showroom or a hotel room so I might get locked into their agenda. It became a cat-and-mouse game, one I won most of the time. When you're in your space, you control the time, interruptions, and your goals for the meeting. As a buyer, it is important never to become too comfortable when in the seller's space. Budget your time, have a series of written expectations for the meeting, and take good notes. Don't make any final buying decisions while together with the presenter. Take away all you need to know and proceed to do your thinking, budgeting, and decision-making in your own space and time.

Manage expectations

As a manager, your role as the buyer carries a great deal of weight. It's important that you understand the value of your position inside the organization: your customers and sales team look forward to your next decision. Every customer looks forward to products that are new, exciting, and fresh. You're also responsible for creating interest and enthusiasm for what's next.

As we have witnessed all throughout the pandemic, most goods showed up late, if at all. Marketing was also slowed until a clearer picture emerged, indicating when we might be able to do more than shop for groceries. Timing is essential between the buyer and the marketing folks. If new product marketing appears too early, consumer enthusiasm can wane quickly. Your job is to manage expectations, including stoking internal fires in your sales team. Creating a complete picture for those responsible for sales will help assure success right as goods hit the floor.

As the head cheerleader, you want to keep up with your supplier teams on all new arrivals. Your role is to communicate the key features and the reasons to own the product. Being a buyer is much more than approving sales orders. Managing expectations is an important piece of creating the enthusiasm and energy necessary for sales success, no matter the quality of your choices.

YOUR EXPECTATIONS

Before you step into any meeting where negotiations will take place have a well-laid-out number of expectations. Sit down and write out your list of expectations. What do you want to see happen? What is not acceptable? What should be off the table from the start? Adding a new supplier or product category can take time, with a great deal of back and forth. Suppliers want to push more products and more categories every chance they get. They have one way of looking at opportunity. On the other hand, you have many suppliers and commitments. You also have inventory limitations.

Set the tone early by laying out what is possible. By knowing your expectations, you can control the direction and tone of any meeting. In a first meeting, both sides are gathering facts while not providing too many specifics. Your job is to pull out from the supplier exactly what they want and what they are willing to give up. Be clear with what you may be looking for from the other side. If the supplier is unwilling to meet even your basic demands, you can save a lot of time by ending the session. Chances are, they will return with more of what you want. If not, there are many suppliers. Never appear too eager or needy; you're in charge. You own the purchase order and the decision.

STANDARDS

You're in charge. You manage a key category of the operation. Certainly, the organization has a set of standards for everyone to follow. You should have your own set of standards for your department and your supplier relationships. These standards become your guideposts for how you run your department. You need to communicate these standards to every supplier. These standards set the tone for how you operate your department. They establish how you want to be treated and how you will treat others. Put them in writing. Refer to them often, especially at the start of the buying season.

Before you create your standards, look at your organization's standards. See where you can find commonality between the rules and your expectations. You certainly want to keep in step with the rules already in place. It is a good idea to review and update your standards once a year to always remain current with the organization as well as standard industry practices.

Pressure

Your role comes with a full plate of stress and pressure. As the person responsible for helping the organization achieve both sales and margin targets, you sit in the sweet spot of specific assumptions throughout the year. So it's important to develop a process for how you manage your day, including those pressures. You can step back and slow things down as needed. Decisions, especially those involving large orders or new vendors, should be made deliberately, with much planning and prep. Develop and borrow best practices from leaders you admire. There will be targets and timelines to meet, so it's within your capacity to manage your work and deliver it on time. Never worry about pressure from the supplier side. It has been my experience that once you slow things down in any negotiation or walk away, suppliers will back down, fearful of expulsion from the process. As the decision maker, you have your hands directly on the controls. Learn the hot buttons for each salesperson. Learn their tone, body language, and mood swings, and then determine how best to manage the next steps. Lay out your work for the day and prioritize those items that will move the needle for the organization. Be cool and never allow a future buying decision to create stress or sleepless nights. And walk away when you have to: you're in control. Enjoy the journey, but don't take the work or yourself too seriously.

Cheerleader

An important part of your job is to always champion your decisions. Once you commit to a new supplier, category, or product lineup, you are now the head cheerleader who will sell with the greatest energy. Work with your supplier partners to devise a strategy that will create enthusiasm for what's coming.

First, it's essential to educate and excite your salespeople to create that initial success. Strong sales in the first few weeks are critical to success, both in the short and long term. After your time with the internal sales staff, work with marketing on a plan for the introduction and a longer-term strategy. That means developing an ongoing plan for ads and social media exposure. Frequent communication is critical. Never miss the chance to talk about the new product, especially touting any early successes. Add a sales contest to keep the energy and enthusiasm. Contests are always better when you partner with the supplier, having them share or handle the costs. Buying is the action; cheerleading helps create and support your success.

When in doubt

Suppliers are always looking to sell you something. You therefore need an additional tool for your toolbox: a filter that helps you to separate truth from an overpromise. I have even seen a buyer's manager put pressure on them to accept a deal from a supplier. As you gain more experience, there will be times when you feel it may be the right or absolute wrong time to buy. There will be other times when you just cannot decide.

When I was in doubt, I would push pause on a negotiation. It wasn't a flat-out No, but it told the supplier my organization was not ready or convinced that we should move ahead. I would then dig deeper, into the proposal and the real opportunity. The pause was not only about putting the supplier on ice, I wanted to see how the supplier would respond. What might they be willing to do to get me back in a room? How would they sweeten the proposal? My issue always came down to one thing: will my team be able to sell the product?

Take the time necessary to listen to your head and feel your gut when choosing your next move. Push back on any supplier who goes above you in order to get a deal done. (It happens.) Weigh the pros and cons of every program. When in doubt, yes is never the answer, until you can solve any angst you feel. If every buyer had the chance to write a book, I'd bet that 90% of their regrets would be on the goods they should not have purchased instead of on the omissions that turned out to be winners Success fades, while regret sticks around like gum on your shoe. Take the time to get it right.

Never settle

As you prepare for a supplier meeting, you will create a series of goals that you must have to complete any deal. There are also the wish list goals, the extraordinary items that provide maximum benefit inside any program. Throughout my career as a buyer, no supplier ever added perks or benefits to a program we were working to complete. It was my job to understand both sides of the negotiation and then to work to get what I needed for my organization. The supplier, on the other hand, is doing their homework and working through a minimal offer they believe you might accept.

Buying is negotiating with a lot of back and forth. You may not get everything you want, but it's your job to ask for it. Your goal is to get everything you want while giving up as little as you can. Some negotiations take time, so you must decide if the fight is worthwhile and the supplier is important to your business. No matter how much energy you spend, never settle just to complete a program. In the end, fight to get all you can, or end the conversation and walk away.

Adding flavor

As the buyer, you get to make the final choice on the products your people sell. No matter your industry, think beyond the everyday purchase. Think past the first item your customers want to own. The add-on purchase is a critical part of any transaction, whether in the store or online. Think beyond the standard presentation and look at the new and unique items that can drive purchases. Adding flavor means going beyond those goods that are part of a routine transaction.

Get out of the routine by thinking about your best customers, the top 20%. These are your most profitable customers. They're the ones who most like your business and products. They're also the most willing to add more items to their cart. The key is to show them new and different things that may grab their attention

When you do present new and different products, it may take time for customers to buy into the new direction. Stay the course. It always takes time to reeducate even your best customers. The more they like, the more they will buy. Never give up on adding flavor to your mix.

Your top 20%

The Pareto Principle, also called the 80/20 rule, is named after economist Vilfredo Pareto. The Pareto Principle says that 80% of consequences result from 20% of the causes. I have tested this law and have found it to be sound. I have used it to guide me in my buying decisions, as well as the level of inventory I kept on hand. Let's look at a few 80/20 scenarios within the framework of a buyers' position:

- 80% of sales come from 20% of the products.
- 80% of sales come from 20% of your customers.
- 80% of sales are made by 20% of your team.
- 80% of sales come from 20% of your suppliers.

To become more precise in your decisions look to:

- Identify the top 20% of your sales team. Treat them extraordinarily well. The company that treats every producer the same will eventually lose.

- Identify your top suppliers. Look to build more profitable programs in the future with these brands that produce your best results.

- Identify your top items and develop a never-out program for every key product you buy.

- Most important, identify your best customers, the top 20% who like your organization, products, and people. Look to build them up. Look to never let them down.

In my opinion, it is essential to treat your top customers and producers in extraordinary ways. If these people left you, what would your business become? Paying attention to your top items is the everyday key to driving consistent business. Paying extraordinary attention to your top producers and top spenders, treating each as a unique and valuable star, is the fairest, most incredibly important thing you can do for your business.

SEARCH FOR KNOWLEDGE

As one grows in experience and success, the world is also changing in thousands of ways. During the 30 years I spent as a buyer, I searched high and low for merchandise not only to interest my customers but to excite them as well. I realized over time that learning and getting better in the role would help me retain my value to potential employers in my later years.

Knowledge and skills would become valuable currency. I realized that sitting in my office, studying daily sales and inventory reports, was not adding to my buyer IQ. I realized that the value of acquiring new skills, while honing established skills was an important part of my new self-developing curriculum. Visiting suppliers was also important. Being around top-level executives from several organizations was a great investment of my time.

In addition to adding to my information base, these trips added to my network of valuable contacts. Everyday experience and success can take you only so far. Learning is now a cradle-to-grave exercise that has value, no matter your role. You will never arrive at a place where your education is complete. Even with artificial intelligence on the doorstep, it's vital to keep searching and adding skills to your toolbox. While we may see many jobs disappear, there will always be opportunities for those with curiosity, passion, and experience.

THE DIGITAL AGE

My role as a buyer began with the era of the Apple II personal computer. My wife and I purchased one for our then-8-year-old son, who never looked back. There are so many skills to develop and sharpen as you grow into your role. At the top of the list is understanding the systems that manage your business. You won't be asked to take over a role in the IT department, but it's important to understand the software and become comfortable using the back-of-house systems your organization relies on. People change roles more often than ever, so it's vital to understand all that is changing in software, apps, and overall business technology. It's been said that no matter your industry, all companies are technology companies. Spending time with people who manage the back of the house can provide you with a framework of the things you will need to know for the future. You need to continue being a strong buyer, but you need to add this critical detail to your toolbox.

TRAVEL

Make time to be away from your office on a regular basis. Being out with team members in the field is an important part of building trust and credibility for yourself and your programs. Develop a schedule of buying shows as a way to search for unique products as well as build a professional network. Shows and events can be a major influence on your growth as you touch small brands and meet industry leaders. Also, look to visit competitors throughout a region or even throughout the country. Ideas are everywhere and moving beyond your office can develop your curiosity in new ways. Your career is about development as much as it is about execution. Take advantage of every opportunity to see new places, meet new people, and be exposed to new things that are different from your regular life. Touching new experiences can and will make you a better buyer. Building a powerful contact list can offer a lifetime of friendship and connection. No matter if you're traveling to a store, a show, or a supplier's headquarters, understanding each one is a chance to grow professionally.

TECHNOLOGY

In order to grow your success, you need to embrace the latest technology your organization is using. Although I talk about having a gut feeling in decision-making, the buying world is dominated by spreadsheets, data, EDI, and other technologies that give businesses a leg up in making better choices. From new software, new apps, and the latest mobile point of sale, it's important to embrace the new tools purchased and coveted by your employer. With buyers being in the bullseye of change, you need the knowledge and comfort of these new tools. Technology is something you always want to keep in front of you. The fastest way to extinction in a role is by ignoring change. Make the IT team your best friends. Any company that plans to play a role in the future of business must continue to update its technology. That's your call to action to take the time to learn all you can about the business of your business.

GREAT BUYERS

Becoming a top-flight buyer takes time, patience, a lot of meetings, and several mistakes. Buyers are special people because they have a discipline and a care for their organization which is both unique and special. Working with great buyers is both a privilege and an education. They simply know how to get it done.

Lesson learned: From the author

Being a buyer means you're constantly in learning mode. There are always new circumstances and situations that will test your skills and experience. The term "buyer beware" is an important phrase to remember any time you need to make a significant purchase. Being patient when others are not is important as well. Digging deep into an opportunity and learning the critical points are essential before you make a decision. Buying for an organization is an honored position. No matter how long you have the opportunity to do it, know that each day is a new day in school.

As our organization grew in size, it became necessary to buy more and more merchandise, including significant amounts of off-price products. One summer I wanted to purchase 500 pairs of shoes, all at a deep discount. I told the sales rep I had an interest in purchasing this number of pairs. He told me If I ordered 500 pairs, I may only receive 200 because they were closeouts. He told me that's how it worked with his organization — there were no guarantees, except that the customer owned the product, whether the product was as ordered or not. I argued not to order some crazy amount, believing they just might ship to that number. After several conversations, I ordered 1,000 pairs, with the expectation of receiving half that number.

You can guess what happened: we received 997 pairs of closeouts. The problem you may not guess is that in addition to this crazy total, we received many bad sizes. The size run favored small, narrow men's feet. These I did not need. In the end, the supplier provided no help. We had to absorb the shoes and then take a loss on the many poor sizes that just didn't work for our customers."

Preparation

"Everyone has a plan 'till they get punched in the mouth."

Mike Tyson.

The buyer is the hunted. Although the buyer is on the offensive, many times searching for the best program or deal, they must also play defense. They need to be aware of what's being sent their way. The best protection from making a buying mistake is being prepared with important details for every supplier meeting. While the buyer may be in need, they must also be wary of everything being presented. The detail of what to have ready is included later. The critical point is to be prepared for the next meeting. Being careful and deliberate are important to acquiring the programs you want minus the items you do not need. Having the data and information that only your side can gather presents an invaluable advantage in any presentation.

What keeps you up

Big jobs come with big worries. Over my career, I had plenty of worries, doubts, and sleepless nights that became part of my decision-making. A number of things can create stress, angst, and worry. Why? None of these things will answer your questions or provide comfort. My experience tells me (and you) it's a waste of good rest to worry about these things. I learned by watching the smartest people in the room that I should be completely prepared, engage fully with the people I was meeting with, get comfortable, be confident, and always be smiling. If you are prepared to move forward and execute the next moves, there is no reason to be staring at the ceiling at 3:00 AM. Prepare before your meetings. Do the necessary research and homework. As you gain experience, you will enjoy a more restful sleep with great results once the sun comes up.

Ever-changing field

A buyer's role is always changing. New brands, product categories, and thought leaders enter the industry, disrupting the status quo. It happens so often that disruption is the status quo.

With ever-increasing reams of data, fewer people in support roles, and fewer dollars to infuse the infrastructure, work requires more time and energy to produce better results. You must move along with the changes. Just as a quarterback must lead the receiver, throwing the ball ahead of the receiver,, you need to consider all of the ways to advance your knowledge of your industry and position. Creating success as a buyer means more than surpassing monthly or quarterly targets. It means striving hard to gain the knowledge today that you will need tomorrow. Step back at times to see where your industry is headed and where your career can go. Dig to gain the knowledge that will help you grow in the least amount of time.

Grow to become the smart buyer

The way to success in the 21st century is through education and knowledge. Some people do well in the classroom, while others learn through hard knocks and everyday ups and downs. If you are a full-time buyer, or if purchasing is part of your job description, work thoroughly to understand all aspects of the role. Get to know the industry, your supplier options, competitors, your customers, and the team that surrounds you. It's important first, to understand the inner workings of your organization. Can you say you know how your company operates on a daily basis? Get to know the people who pull the levers from the inside.

It's also essential to learn about the industry that you navigate through on a daily basis. This includes meeting frequently with suppliers and their sales managers. This will provide you with information you rarely hear just sitting at your desk. The more leaders you know, the greater the options going forward.

Deeper education also comes through books, relevant podcasts, and keeping a personal journal. These will continue to offer great insight and confidence as you pick your own brain for the ways to manage a difficult decision.

Develop listening skills and a more disciplined approach to negotiating. Timely follow-up is also a part of becoming a valuable executive. Follow-up is an all-star asset, given very little air time by most organizations. Finally, work to become the nicest person in the room. Successful people can do business with anyone, but they especially want to do business with nice people.

Homework

Being a good buyer means having the right questions to ask as well as being fully prepared for meetings with suppliers. Before each meeting, you will need to do the necessary prep work to be ready for the easy parts of the conversation and those parts that require a more forceful attitude. Having the essential details is critical to laying the groundwork for you to score a great win for your side. Facts and numbers are key ingredients for successful supplier meetings. Opinions and hearsay will rarely get you the best deal. I have learned that having three years of historical data can help you gain a solid understanding of a supplier's past performance. Because there are many variables, including weather, the supply chain, and the overall economy, this length of detail will provide a strong picture for you. Details to include in your prep homework should include:

- Sales by item, by month.
- Current inventory by item.
- Age of product by item.

- Open order information.

You'll want to know the specific history of this supplier within your organization. As you prepare for the meeting, also spend time on your competitors' websites, searching for product details from your supplier. What is the current status and value of this brand to your customers? Since you will be spending future dollars, you need to make the best future decisions, no matter the levels of past success. The supplier has arrived to warm your heart and make you feel like a Million-dollars. Your mission is to decide if you will go forward, and then to write the best possible deal. Doing the necessary homework is one of your best weapons.

MEETING PREP

As you prepare to meet with an established or prospective supplier, you need a prioritized menu of your expectations. This menu should include:

- Desired price discounts.
- Dating terms.
- Freight concessions.
- Industry-specific advantages.
- Rebates.
- No-charge products.
- The ability to return poor-selling products.

Have these items in writing if you want to make them appear in a program. Review the menu and rehearse each discussion point. Know that in the heat of battle, especially with a major vendor, it's easy to forget even the important wants. No matter the speed or tone of the meeting, it's important to control the pace and the conversation. Preparation is essential, yet underrated. Do all you can to create the best questions and the most complete picture, as well as understand your future needs before your supplier enter the room.

NUMBERS

The constant refrain I hear about sales success says, "You are only as good as your numbers." Certainly, in sales, driving sales every day matters. In purchasing, it's about the buyer knowing their numbers every day, hands down, with no exceptions. From open orders to sales by item, to current inventory, you need to understand the business, beginning with the critical numbers. As you prep for a supplier meeting, you will want to know how this supplier is working for your organization. What is selling and what is not working? Review these critical numbers at the start of your day. Look for trends: What is moving fast? What is taking up valuable space? When your suppliers see your nimbleness with the numbers, they will realize how serious you are. They'll also understand that being open and upfront with you is the way to do business. Knowing the numbers makes you formidable. It's one way you can build inventory and supplier strategies that will work long-term for your business.

THE PRODUCT

Product is the story for every buyer. The mission is to find the right goods, the best price, in the proper quantities, exactly when needed. You are also supposed to deliver on new items, hot items that will turn heads, build traffic, and create sales. Simply put, your job is based on product.

On the surface, buying sounds fairly simple. You pick goods, negotiate the best deal, and have them delivered when needed. But this is the fairy tale version of the role. Acquiring products as you need them takes skill and communication, all to ensure you will get what you expect, when you expect it. While you have your plan for what to purchase, the supplier has a different plan for what they want to see you buy. It's essential you come into any meeting with a plan. It's OK, however, to also come in with an open mind and at least listen to their pitch. Within every meeting, stay true to your plan, listen to the pitch, and then adjust the total spend based on what you like. Know that organizations get into trouble when the inventory is too high, too old, and just wrong for their particular customer. Managing that product makes you a star or not. Stay close to the information and manage the supplier network as you manage the product.

Decisions are yours to make

For many years, companies used focus groups to dig into the minds of consumers: searching for every right answer as they bring new products to market. Thanks to technology and constant product updates, organizations decided to go another way. With technology-advancing cars, smartphones, and even sports equipment far beyond the imagination, asking consumers what they might want in a future product no longer made sense as many new features were far beyond the imagination of the everyday user.

Turn the story onto your page, where the product decisions rest with you. As the buyer, you set the pace. You will want to know what is going on in the wider marketplace. Stretching your view and focusing on the categories you purchase will help you come up with new suppliers and decisions different from anything a focus group might show you.

A solid buying decision is borne of experience, knowledge, detailed homework, and preparation. It also comes from being burned a time or two, investing in products that did not produce solid results. Each purchase brings new knowledge and experience. Make decisions knowing you have done all you can to be prepared for what's next.. The only time you might be afraid of a decision is when you have not prepared. Be confident in your choices, and then work like the devil to help your team sell the product and make money doing it.

Negotiations: the details

There are things you must have in any new program. These items are on your most wanted list, sitting right there in front of you. There are other things: items you hold back or keep in your pocket. These are extraordinary items, the things you might bring up if talks are going well for your side. There are always some things you want but cannot have. Both parties know that neither side gets to eat the entire elephant in the first year of a program.

I would work to grab every asset I could, knowing that I would not score 100%. Once the deal was done I realized the pressure was on me to push my team. We had to work to create extraordinary results so that my next negotiations would give me much more of the assets I wanted for my organization. This worked time after time, as we pushed through the fear the suppliers had, believing we were more talk than results.

Once we produced extraordinary results, the programs got better and better because the supplier trusted us. It's always important to ask for all you can and then more. It's also important to know that at some point your organization will need to produce on results promised. Throughout my years as a buyer, I signed only one-year agreements, knowing I could gain more because the results would fall in line. What are the items to negotiate at a minimum? Here is the starter list.

- Product discounts off wholesale: a minimum of 10%.
- A back-end rebate, based on sales results, paid in cash or free product.
- Freight concessions of X.
- The permission to return X% of the buy, based on unsold goods.
- A marketing allowance in dollars, in order to promote the new goods.

There is more to this list, based on the supplier, your size, and the industry. It's critical that both your team members and your customers are versed on the incoming goods. Both must understand the product's value. If it doesn't meet your criteria, walk away. There is never a reason to buy, promote, or present products that make little sense to your business. Every supplier and every item should have extraordinary reasons for owning space in your world.

NEGOTIATING FOR HIGHER GROUND

Beyond that starter list of items to negotiate, there are additional assets that many suppliers have shown only to certain customers, based on volume. These are items that the supplier keeps under lock and key until they know where the conversation is headed. Although the items are too many to list, and many times exclusive only to certain industries, here a few common add-ons.

- Cash: payment to be able to play in your world, with your team.

- Payment for floor space. This can be in the form of free products.

- Anticipation: payment discounts when invoices are paid early.

- Freight: although COVID has changed everything, free freight was often an extraordinary perk for larger accounts.

- Co-op programs for marketing dollars.

- Contests and incentives for the sales team to assist in selling the products.

- Celebrity appearances. Some industries have sports stars or other influencers to help draw crowds. These people may endorse a supplier brand. This can be a real win-win.

It's important to understand that suppliers will not volunteer additional perks unless required. If there is a risk of a No or an extraordinary push from the buyer, these will remain hidden. It will be up to you to dig and learn what else is available. Being nice will never gain you more, but being diligent can. Suppliers will give more when they fear a deal will not get done or fear an existing customer will go away. Their job is simple: sell the most SKUs with the most inventory, in return for the fewest concessions. Knowing about these additional benefits takes real investigation, knowledge from your network, and serious stubbornness on your part. Suppliers fear the No, especially when they already have your volume plugged into their budgets.

CLIMBING THE PYRAMID

As I approached my mid-30s, one of my mentors told me that to be considered tops in my position, I needed to be in the top 5% of buyers in my industry. After hearing that from a person I believed in, it became my obsession. For the next 15+ years, I did everything possible to grow into a top-level buyer. As I look back, I realize there are things I would do differently. Here is my list of things to do to grow into a top-flight performer:

- Never stop learning.
- Seek out the current experts who do what you do for their advice.
- Listen to podcasts and attend webinars within your field.
- Try new things. Seek out new directions. Never fear failing up.
- If you lose a job, get back on the horse. Don't sit on the sidelines, contemplating your next move. Jump into a new role where you can learn new things while paying the bills.
- Never stop trying to be the best.

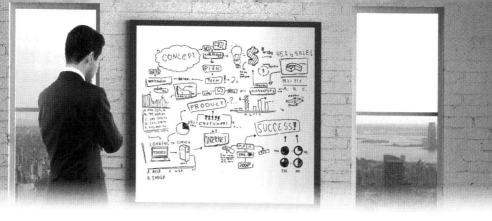

Planning

"A smooth sea never produced a skilled sailor."
Franklin Delano Roosevelt

As noted elsewhere, buying involves managing inventory, a menu of suppliers, delivery schedules, markdowns, and product training. It is a never-ending process of goods going out, goods coming in, and dealing with all of the products customers just don't want to buy.

Although there are slow times and busy times within any industry, there is never a slow period for the buyer. Setting up a season with the best mix of merchandise happens well before the actual season. Plus, he or she must continue to manage the goods already on the shelves. It's an art to becoming a great merchant.

RISKS

As the person responsible for sales, profit, and inventory management, you are under pressure and face many risks: internal margin expectations, purchasing expectations from suppliers, and markdowns if the sales just aren't happening. Good buyers are rarely overwhelmed by it however, because they build and work a plan that includes both an upside and a downside. Organizations value gross margins and expect any purchase to yield strong margins and great sell-through. Selling every item at full markup is not realistic and rarely happens. So a key function is to manage the sell-through, especially once the markdown process begins. How can you work with your suppliers to maximize both sales and margin for the entire life cycle of the inventory?

Managing sell-through is a skill that takes time and experience to get right. On the flip side, you must decide if you should even say yes to a purchase. Do the downside risks hold more sway than any success might create? There is no secret to creating profitable sell-through. It takes good decisions, great communication, and diligence to move products while managing margins. Good buyers do not see heavy traffic ahead, they plan for open roads and sunny skies while preparing for detours. Create your plan and consider the risks. Once you feel good about it, pull the trigger and start to manage the process until the last item is sold.

SMALL BUYS/SMALL TRIES

This book has suggested that every good buyer should be willing to consistently take risks. The idea of offering new ideas and products to your customers will absolutely help your business grow. The inevitable caveat is that the new ideas and products are digestible, easy to manage, and easy to extinguish if things don't work out. Surprises, especially those that include spending money outside the norm, are generally not received well by leadership. Communicating with your manager when you want to try something beyond the ordinary is smart. It's essential to stretch your muscles in order to build better skills and more confidence. Here are a few keys to stretching those muscles.

- Make any test buy small, easy to market, present, and manage.

- Inform your manager, especially at the beginning. This is not about permission, it's just smart business.

- It's vital to gain supplier buy-in on any trial purchase. If you're expected to walk the plank alone, say no.

- Be 100% certain about any small purchase. This is your decision.

- When a test works, exploit the knowledge quickly. You

have interest, you need product.

- When a trial fails, move the goods out, and make note of the event in your journal.

- Understand that a small win is just that. Do not assume you now have license to take larger risks with any new, first-time item.

- The same holds true with failure. No failure should frighten you off.

- Small buys should always play a part in your role, no matter how many locations, or the size of the sales volume. New and risky products deserve a trial, not a full investment.

FROM THE BEGINNING

To provide yourself with the best chance for new product success, front-load all you do to support the new introduction. This should include a full communication plan. Overspend on the front end with your time, energy, and budgeted marketing resources. Creating energy and sales from that first day can mean larger volume and a longer shelve life. Every product, no matter the brand or hype, has a life cycle. Your efforts can extend that life with a strong initial push. Do all you can to build momentum from the start. Your role is to move the energy and enthusiasm from your desk onto your team. Key parts of a successful introduction include:

- Bringing in the supplier to train your sales team on the product before the first delivery.

- Have the social media and marketing plans secured and communicated early.

- Informing the receiving team to get the product out ASAP.

- Promote the presentation on the floor and website,

providing a clear, colorful message.

- Measure sales every day, staying in touch with the supplier in order to maximize the partnership effort from the first week of the introduction.

- Make any necessary adjustments in placement, presentation, or marketing as sales drop, or if sales numbers are less than expected.

To increase your odds of success for every new program, put your best assets forward at the start. Don't take a wait-and-see approach. If an overstock requires extra help down the line, ask the supplier to support a different promotion. Get your ducks in a row at the beginning in order to build the groundwork for success and long shelf life.

MAKE IT SIMPLE

Creating the easiest path to purchase should be a major priority for the entire leadership team. The world is loud, busy, and complex. If you make buying a complex process, expect people to leave empty-handed. Work constantly on making the customer's buying process seamless. Attention spans are shorter than ever, so getting people to visit your location or visit your website is a grand first step. The trick is to make these next steps informational, fun, and fast. Creating a sale is more difficult than ever, from the product story to your internal education, presentation, pricing, and signage. The combative noise against you and your product is overwhelming. It's important to have a product people can see, touch, demo, and learn about in the shortest amount of time possible. It's important to reach out to every team member, ask questions, and gain new ideas. Because every team member is a consumer, they'll provide direct feedback on aspects of the presentation and the road to purchase. The goal is to make the buying experience simple and fast. Be the leader that brings good ideas to life. Communicate that mission in order to sell more goods, more often, as well as create more add-on sales.

SEARCH, FAR AND WIDE

When it came to the subject of products, I had two priorities. 1) To have the core, essential items always in stock. And 2) to always be searching for new products that would create enthusiasm and sales. Buying is much more than saying yes to a purchase order. It's the art of telling inviting stories and adding new items that drive traffic and sales. As the product leader, it's important to set the tone and the environment in your locations, whether physical or virtual.

As you create a reputation for having the location that will always present the latest in your elected categories, your customers will budget more time on their calendars to visit. Buying is doing the basic actions that will keep goods in stock. Buying is also searching and researching what might be hot in the future. Once a quarter, look at your product categories to see which ones need enhancement. Be sure to spend the necessary time, listening to your sales team. Provide energy and enthusiasm during slow periods. Talk to them about their ideas about brands and products. Your search can only get better once you know where you want to be. Sales are driven by the everyday basics while margins can be greatly enhanced with the new products you discover.

NEVER IGNORE THE NEXT WINNER

After my years as a buyer ended, I began to work in sales management roles, selling to both regional and national accounts. It immediately became an act of frustration, however, in my simple attempt to book an appointment to introduce the brand and product. The brands I represented were either new or not well-known. We had small marketing budgets, so they acquired few eyeballs. I confess that as a young buyer, I gave little time to small, challenger brands that wanted a place on my calendar.

Thirty-five years ago, my industry had fewer brands, with the big brands owning much of the market share. Although I was guilty of not paying attention to those small brands, I was not committing a great sin. Today, new ideas and brands are arriving all the time, with great products within these brands. Frankly, they deserve some time on your calendar. I recommend you meet with three to five new brands every quarter. Provide each with a 20-minute pitch window in order to share their story. Although you will not support every one, you will find a few exciting products that will grow your business. Every brand begins as a dream. Even the largest today took decades, a lot of money, and extraordinary talent to grow. New brands have little access to any of these assets. They have to work hard just to gain an inch or two. A 20-minute meeting will provide these folks great energy, while possibly providing you a shot at the next great winner. Every brand begins with no market share and few successes. Why not look at these second-tier brands that just may have the next great product?

"THINK TIME"

Suppliers are constantly knocking on your door, eager to tell you about their new amazing products. Your team is also looking to you for solutions. Even when you're alone, there are people swirling in your head, attempting to change your mind. To give yourself a bit of space, delegate anything and everything that is not about you or your department. Send these headaches to others on the team to solve.

Next, clean up your calendar of those people who are not part of your mission. Doing your job well takes time, effort, and space. Never allow others to steal these assets in order to relieve their own pain. Carve out "think time" for yourself. Every manager should carve out quiet time to think deeply about the work and ways to make it better. It's about finding your own place away from the noise and without interruption. It could include a daily walk, a quiet drive, or maybe time in a small coffee shop where you are looking only for ideas, answers, and maybe a latte. Stepping away on a regular basis can give you the chance to exercise your most important work tool, your brain. This is not about a break or sick time. It is the chance to apply your experience, knowledge, and skills to old problems and new ideas. Getting away to get better at what you do is a very important business practice. Think time should be part of your success strategy.

The ingredients: a quiet place, a notebook, and a pen. Leave the phone and laptop somewhere else. Put it in your calendar, in order to make it real for you and everyone else.

Execution

> "You don't have to be the smartest person in the room, but you do need to know who is."
>
> Indra Nooyi

Each day, the buyer attacks their to-do list, moving through it with deliberation. This is where the best buyers excel, where they juggle several balls all while managing their day with excellence. From communicating with internal teams to managing the calendar, buyers possess the ability to think beyond the norm. Success doesn't happen every day, but experienced buyers know how to manage the accompanying stress. They have a knack for doing many things well, all while working not to make poor decisions.

SELL-THROUGH: IT'S WHAT MATTERS

During my career, I have met many buyers and suppliers who are all about the arrival of new products. Once the order is placed, they work together to prepare for the products to arrive and position them in a prime location. Preparing for a new presentation can be fun and exciting. Surely, the buyer must continue to offer new products to his team and customer throughout the buying season. That initial excitement is not the main story for the buyer or the organization. That initial yes, together with the new goods hitting the floor, is only 30% of the buyer's work. You're not paid to just stock the shelves. Your role is about the entire plan, most of

it beyond the initial program purchase. That plan should include:
- Product pricing strategy.
- Marketing as well as a social media schedule.
- Presentation and display set up.
- Training program for the internal sales team.
- The markdown strategy and schedule.

Every product has a life cycle. The product at first is new and shiny, but in time, it gets picked over and purchased to its specific level of popularity, then moves to the markdown phase. Every buy must include the above elements. And the buyer must concentrate just as much on the entire sell-through piece as the introduction of any new product or category. If an initial buy has great success, timely replenishment is the next step. If the initial introduction is a flop, then the buyer needs a robust plan B. If, after a reboot, the product is not selling, get with the supplier to build a fast exit strategy. This is the part where your supplier can provide assistance in the form of energy, and financial help. In the end, sales with margin matter. You will be judged by the total numbers you produce, not by the front end of a sales program.

RESULTS

How did you land your current role? What steps led you to the world of buying? How did your predecessor do the job? Finally, if today was your first day on the job, how might you build beyond the expectations of the organization? You gain experience with each passing day. At times, however, people tend to get lost in the minutia of their work. Let's call it the busy work we each need to perform throughout the week.

Your role is about making the best decisions you can in bringing products to your website or retail outlets. It's about the right products arriving on time and in the right amounts.

Results matter. Achieving the benchmarks set by the organization is the reason to get out of bed every day. As you review your to-do list, always push the low-priority items aside and concentrate on the key results you're expected to deliver. Anything not part of leadership's expectations can wait for another time. As you prepare for the next day, prioritize the things that matter: sales, inventory, margins, sell-through rates, and distressed inventory. All the work needs to get done, but not all of this work is the priority. Prioritize what is vital to your customers and organization.

CHOOSING THE FINEST FRUIT

Top brands provided amazing products that my customers wanted to buy. Although several of the suppliers were vital to our success, the number of items that were essential to our success was surprisingly low. Take a thorough look at your buying plan. You have a limited time to buy, so your spending must be always about those items that drive your success. If you're purchasing products in several categories, buy the key items in each of those categories. Just because a supplier offers you several items beyond their top categories, never clog up an order with low-priority items. Allow each supplier to provide the items that are key for your organization. Suppliers insist on more items on their sales orders. They have their A, B, and C products. So pick the A and maybe a few B items only. Even top brands have many weak items in their catalog. So stay away from programs that force you to take products that make little sense to your business. At the same time, avoid favors to a sales rep. It happens a great deal. Doing favors is bad business. Buy what you need, and then negotiate what others want you to buy.

CURIOSITY

To be successful, a buyer must be curious. They need to search far and wide for that next amazing item that will turn heads and make the cash register sing. Being curious, while sharpening your search skills, will help you remain at the top of your game. Be curious about how to attract and sell more.

There are a few very important words that have remained constant for decades. "New" is one that grabs the eye. With an economy driven in large part by the consumer, "New" and

"Unique" are important words that should be associated with any product search. Spark that curiosity and search for those special items that create wide smiles. Curiosity will enable you to remain an important and relevant buyer.

WHAT IF #2

You said no to a large deal that checked every one of your boxes. There will be times when things look good but just won't add up in your head. If you have done your due diligence, it's OK to step back. Maybe the answer should be No, or "not right now." Feel good about your actions. Buying can be a lonely role. There are few people who know what you know or think as you think. When things just don't seem right to you, your instincts are telling you something. Even if it's just to reexamine the offer, don't second-guess the decision. Never worry about blowback from suppliers. Yes, they have put time, effort, and expense into their offer, but that has no bearing on your decision. It's their job. If your answer is No, then say so without fear of reprisal. If a deal is right, it will show itself to you.

I have been here many times. Every buyer has agonized over programs versus people. Never say yes for the sake of the relationship. Every decision you make has consequences. You must believe in the deal first in order to make it work. Each must fit into your plans.

THE TRIAL

You're close to agreeing to a large new program with a key supplier. But you're not comfortable with the amount of product it requires you to purchase. If you like most of the plan, step back and run a test. Purchase a few dozen units, or whatever makes sense. Although you will be buying these test items at the regular price, be sure to price them at the agreed-upon program price. Test them in a few locations.

If they sell well, you can confidently move forward with the larger program. If the products never take off, you've made a great decision while saving the organization from making a real mistake. Being a successful buyer includes making decisions like this. While you are paid to buy, promote, and sell products at high margins, you are also expected to manage inventory levels. A trial can help you make better decisions, avoid supplier pressure, and help keep inventory levels in check all season long.

BAD BUYS

During my years as a buyer, I put as much time and effort into purchases that never took off, as well as those that became winners. You will, too. But don't worry, buyers develop over time. From the time you begin, you're in a constant growth program.

In the beginning, buyers are cautious, moving slowly and double-checking their plans. They will go for the products they know will sell, even if the margins are less than expected. A new buyer knows one thing for certain: the goods must sell.

As they mature, they'll go into deeper waters and greater risks, believing now they can feel when a deal is right. Good buyers believe in themselves and their actions. Some buys will have poor results, no matter the homework you do. It's essential to recognize the bad buy, communicate it to the sales team, and put a plan in place to flush out the goods that are not moving on their own. Talk to your team and your manager for suggestions. When others participate, they will own more of the process. Bad buys will happen; manage them, and then move on.

THE OTHER SIDE OF BUYING

Over thirty years, I woke up preparing to spend someone else's money. It was great fun and a great challenge. I chose what to buy and how much. It was all within my hands. I created product menus for each employer that would appeal to their specific customer base. Even though it was all in the same industry and categories, products change due in large part to technology. That made many decisions difficult and time-consuming.

Most times, the products sold well. In those times when the opposite was true, I had to find solutions. Moving out poor sellers, freeing up cash, and preparing for better decisions were all important parts of my role.

There are times you will build a sell-off solution. Other times, you will need to bring in the supplier in order to eliminate the poor inventory. No matter the path, it's vital that you be involved and even spearhead the plan. Since you have leverage with the supplier network, you will get better results than those who do not sign the purchase orders. Know that 30% of the work is the purchase while 70% is everything else.

Inventory nightmares

There are times when everyone seems busy, other times when the team takes their collective eye off the ball, or in this case, off the inventory. Inventory can and does get out of control. Sales slow down, yet open orders are allowed to ship, adding to the nightmare. Many times, goods can also arrive late, too deep into the selling season to make a difference. The list of nightmares can be endless. There is now too much inventory and too little time left in the season. Here are some solutions based on extensive experience:

- Stop all purchases, except for paid-in-full special orders.

- Hold or cancel all open orders.

- Dig in to understand the exact problem and detail on overages. Do not accept hearsay.

- Get together with your manager and the sales team to bring all into the conversation.

- This group should devise a plan to eliminate overstocks quickly and painlessly.

- Manage total gross margins as the organization flushes through the overstocks.

- Search for some deeply-discounted products you know you can buy and sell at huge margins to offset the sell-off.

- Set the plan, explain the urgency, and remain focused

until the goods are gone.

Identifying the problem is a great first step. The moment you have your arms around the entire scope of the problem, it should remain part of the daily effort until the overstocks are gone. It's important to focus on the specific items that are the issue. The total inventory is not out of line, only certain items. Decide if this should be an internal solution or one that needs your supplier's help. Build the solution, communicate it, and put it into motion.

OFF-PRICE PRODUCTS

I have watched several great operators build their businesses around off-priced goods. Some people consider these items mistakes that just never worked, others believe every product has a lifecycle and some just linger too long. And there are customers who want to own the hot new item on the first day, while others will wait until that same item drops to its lowest price.

There are far too many stores and e-commerce sites to search. When you do look at off-price, the selections are broken and missing some of the most popular items. At the same time, the suppliers are looking to move these goods in a hurry.

You can offer some low prices when buying. One suggestion is to start so low, you believe the number to be insulting. They can always say no and you can move higher if you choose. In the end, when you discount these off-priced items just to move them, you'll want to make a gross margin of at least 40%.

Once you decide, write down what you are buying. Hold your supplier to the notion you expect a 100% delivery of this order. Keep score over time. At some point, you will probably end up working with a very small group of people and suppliers regarding off-price goo Many people know how to write an order, but not everyone knows how to keep to the program. Buying off-price goods is meant to be a win-lose, with you and your organization as the big winner.

REPLENISHMENT

The real strength in sales is in replenishment — filling in the popular items as quickly as possible. The first large delivery of a new program is somewhat easy for both the buyer and supplier. Depending on the size of both organizations, reorders are usually done through a digital process or through team members. Replenishment is essential to maintaining any growth throughout the year. No first delivery can be large enough to set up a program for success, no terms can be too long. Reorders create and determine the long-term success of any supplier relationship. Here are a few things to know about replenishment:

- The buyer should oversee and manage this process.

- Work with your IT and accounting people to build an appropriate plan for key suppliers.

- Once a new program is delivered, pull the sales reports for the first three months to determine the speed and frequency of turn for each item.

- Create a never-out program for those items essential to your everyday business.

- Review your replenishment program often. Tweak when necessary.

- Watch sell-through carefully. Customers fall in and out of love. Never get caught on the wrong side of the love.

- Remember that every product has a life cycle. What is bright and shiny today, will turn into just another product in the discount bin tomorrow.

- Customers either want the latest and greatest product or want everything marked down to the floor. The buyer's job is one of reading minds, as well as digesting spreadsheets.

IT'S NOT HARD, IT'S ABOUT EXECUTION

Some people talk a great game yet achieve average or poor results. There are others who come in early, work as hard as they know how, and achieve mediocre results. Many people believe that if they complete everything on their to-do list, the planets will align and create success all around.

In the end none of this matters. What does matter is execution, lining up the square pieces into the square holes. Successful execution is about buying right, communicating to every critical person, managing presentations, observing sell-through, and looking for anything that will help you sell more at higher margins.

For decades, I have wondered how some people continue to collect paychecks for poor results and mediocre sales. Do your job well: Do it on time, and know every product and and result over time. Be kind to your team members. Do the things that excite your team and customers. Seek out problems before they become a crisis. Build a better team as you strive to create a better sales organization.

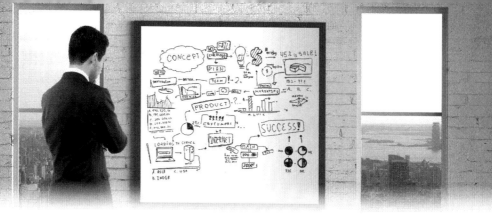

Organization

"If you do the work you get rewarded. There are no shortcuts in life."

Michael Jordan

One of your most important skills is in getting your mind in focus before you approach suppliers. Before the business can move to execution, it must organize a plan. In the sales department, it's your job to get all parts rolling together. Being organized is invaluable, especially when it comes to inventory control. There are any number of things that can go wrong here, and you must have a complete understanding of all potential issues. After shrinkage, breakage, and discounts, margins can become razor-thin. It takes a great deal of work to build a program that will produce results. Being organized is what will help you to succeed.

PRIORITIES

In the course of planning each day, you will decide how to invest your time. You will also decide which people to bring into your day. Here are a few suggestions:

- Every day, create a 5 – 6 item list of major things to accomplish.

- Only allow people with appointments into your day. Walk-ins are often big time wasters.

- As you work through your list, that next open item

becomes your new #1.

- Take time each day to move away from your space. Never allow your calendar to pin you to one place.

- Schedule lunch with different people: suppliers, team members, the manager, and members of your network. Lunch is a time not just to relax and eat, but to build connections.

- Take a walk for 15 – 20 minutes to clear your mind and gain valuable exercise.

You need to understand what is important to your organization and community. Your to-do list should reflect the needs and wants of of each. Learning how to manage your time and being as productive as possible are important to doing the job well. Managing time will help you build a better organization and a more solid reputation, leading to a long and successful career.

Good, better, best

A good buyer does many things. They work each day to outthink their suppliers and to have their inventory catch their customers' eye. As you think about product choices, think about the number three. You want three options, driven by different retail prices, to cast your net around the widest group of customers. Providing three price options not only offers choice, but customers will tend to choose upwards, away from the low option to the middle or best selection available. The differences are certainly greater than just price. It's about the features and benefits that will drive more sales. In your most important product categories, try to always offer three options. Doing this shows that you offer great choice, real value, and quality at several levels. Think good, better, best. Anything less will cost you dollars, anything more may cost you customers. Too many choices are as bad as too few. Good, better, best creates the smartest selection.

Beyond the order

Once the purchase order has been executed, it's time to move to the work beyond, beginning with creating new product codes, speaking with accounting, working with marketing to create a message, and then planning the presentation story. There are many jobs within the job to help drive success. Working with the supplier on a product training schedule for staff is another task that will pay off for months to come. I believe 70% of the buying effort is about tasks executed after the order, which means you must have a system for introducing new products or brands to your team and your customers. New products need to be introduced with a lot of energy and speed. Without these, you may never know why a product wins or loses. Bring your best enthusiasm, energy, and confidence to the launch. Your team is interested and curious, so work to convince your community that these are your best decisions to date.

First things

As you start your day, begin with the following set of actions:

- Review sales by item for the previous day.
- Review the potential markdown list.
- Look at all open orders, including any lingering backorders.
- Review the product aging report.
- Look for trends that may either create overstocks or critical shortages.
- Review your social media schedules and recent results.
- Consider new promotions to help spur sales, and/or move excess product.

During my corporate years, I would run through that list above for all locations. I wanted to know exactly what sold, where they sold, and if there might be best individual practices to uncover. Within the reports, I wanted to see if any locations were doing better than the rest. If some numbers were off the charts, I would make calls to learn more. Reports never tell the complete story. By reaching out to managers and sales leaders, you might find a program or story that can generate more sales in more places.

It's critical to learn where to best spend your time driving success in those locations seeing the best results. Remember the Pareto principle: look at the top 20% of your locations. Investing time where you can help generate greater results will pay off for the present as well as the long term. Locating those engaged team members can be a great return on your time and energy.

REIMAGINE THE BUY

Eighty percent of the U.S. economy is driven by the consumer. From cars to apparel to electronics and beyond, this economy thrives on the next purchase. People want to buy and own the next shiny new thing. They want the latest items to show off to their friends and on their social media outlets.

Once upon a time, there was tremendous loyalty to many different brands in several consumer categories. Today, not so much. Where once, a buyer might overspend to buy large stock in a branded closeout, the smart buyer today takes more of a lean approach. They buy less, move it through, and then buy just a bit more. Other than the large big box stores and some e-commerce locations, big buys are not part of the everyday plan. It's about being lean and showing new products more often to create a great sense of buying urgency. These are the days of frequent, small buys. You may even choose to create several one-and-done offerings, where you buy the item once, sell it out, at top margin and move on.

It's important today to keep your customer excited and motivated. Today's younger, active consumer does not want piles of goods with large discount signs. They want to own the next cool thing. When you create a sense of scarcity, you can build greater traffic, more energy, and receipts with larger totals. The days of bulking up the warehouse are over. Buying is more about studies and trials and more careful replenishment. Consumers move off of products quickly. You never want to get caught running discount promo after discount promo. Watch what your customers are buying in the first few weeks. Look at your competition to see how they deal with their consumers and see what you can learn.

AN ESSENTIAL: SIMPLY STATED

Putting any large deal together is difficult and time-consuming. Negotiating is tough, especially when many people are involved on both sides, many of whom you may not know. One important task I learned over time was to write down every key comment or point spoken. During times where we were negotiating with a key supplier, I asked my administrative assistant to be involved in the meeting. I offered to have these notes shared with everyone involved if they wished. Taking detailed notes is an essential part of the negotiations, especially if there are many strangers in the room. I also found it useful to have everyone introduce themselves in the first meeting, explaining their job and the role they had in these meetings. Confusion can run rampant in a room filled with people doing more speaking than listening. So taking good notes and listening intently to what is being said is valuable. Sharing the notes at the beginning of each meeting can help keep things on track and avoid confusion. Start any negotiations by assisting in setting the tone, keeping things on track, and helping to crystalize the to-do list for everyone. When there is a plan for organization noted at the start, everyone will feel good about the chance to create a true partnership.

SHORTCUTS: CREATING A BETTER DAY

Employers pay for performance that will enable them to grow. There are different ways to do your job. Some buyers take the long route to the target and others simply cut through the woods, trying to do the job in the shortest time. After I had been working for many years, I realized: the work was never going to end. No matter how early I arrived or how late I stayed, that to-do list just seemed to grow and grow, even on those days when I was on fire.

So the goal should be thorough execution of the work every

day. Getting things done on time will help you create a strong reputation, which will become a major résumé point over time.

Another idea: step back from the work once a month or quarter and analyze it. Look at the things you do, how you do your job. Talk to other buyers. Get to understand and then share best practices. You're probably doing things other buyers can also use. The more you get to know other buyers and how they work, the more you might achieve. Continue to seek out the things other companies are doing. Take lunch or coffee meetings with smart buyers in other industries. Drill into the minds of the experts. Learn, copy and use what they do well.

One of the great competitor-copiers was Mr. Sam Walton of Walmart fame. If he could seek out best practices from his competitors, you can certainly do the same. Most will be flattered and happy to share. Be willing to change if what you learn is superior to the way you do things. Never be afraid to grow, change, or ask other smart buyers for their advice.

Management

"There are no traffic jams on the extra mile."
Zig Ziglar

Good buyers know who they're buying from, and will not make any decision until they do their homework. Management is about information, the orders written, and the people awaiting the decisions. Rolling out the plan on paper is another vital part of the buyer's success. This involves doing the gritty details. It's critical to know the steps, write them down, and execute each one as an individual decision that will bring maximum success once all steps are completed.

INFORMATION: THE BASICS

Timely, correct information is one of the fundamentals of being a buyer. Securing accurate information in order to better understand the future will help you make better decisions. As you grow to trust your suppliers, you'll dig for information that goes far deeper than the standard news stories circling your industry. The more you learn, the more your organization benefits. Some details come from your internal sales history from the past three years. With 36 months of purchasing history, sales, and margin reports, you can not only see how things evolved, you can also spot trends. They can tell you stories about your suppliers, products, and price points that will make a difference in your buying decisions. My reports were always far more reliable than my memory. Use the reports that make sense to the future. If there are other things you want to learn, talk to the IT staff about building customized reports. In addition to using the reports, I worked very hard to gather as much competitive intelligence as possible during any meeting with suppliers. Being stuck most weeks in my office meant I needed to rely on supplier information to learn those important stories happening beyond my walls. Just remember that no matter who provides the details, take any and all incoming information with a grain of salt.

Purchase orders

Keep a record of every order you place. It not only builds a record of what is real, you're also creating a record for every key member of your organization. Although you may believe in your supplier network, mistakes happen. There is also that rare case where an order is padded with a few extra items. You may even experience a phantom order showing up, one you knew nothing about. Once written, that purchase order circulates to every internal department including accounting, sales, receiving, as well as the supplier.

When the order arrives, the receiving and accounting staff will match up what you ordered against the receiving document and the invoice. Every purchase order has a unique number, which helps you track the order, especially when things go wrong. The PO should also include the items ordered, date requested, cancel date, costs, discounts, payment terms, and instructions about backorders. You will use the POs to follow every purchase and speed of delivery. It keeps the key people in the loop and provides instructions in case things go wrong. Before an order is placed, it is a good habit to check all open orders to see if what you want to order is not on a previous sales order.. Finally, no matter the size of the order or dollar amount, always provide a purchase order. That decision will save you a lot of headaches.

Purchase order detail

It's essential to communicate your purchasing rules to every supplier, detailing every important point on the PO. Setting direction in writing ensures every order is managed to the expectations you have set. If not, others may create their own standards for you. No matter your method, be certain to provide written instructions to each supplier for accepting, shipping, and billing orders. Provide this detail to every sales rep to ensure your wishes have been communicated. Below are several points to consider when putting together your requirements for your supplier network:

- Position the purchase order number on packing slips and all invoices.

- Allow no product substitutions without your written approval.

- Accept no backorders or no back orders beyond 30 days of the order date.

- Have a firm cancellation date for every order.

- Include complete shipping instructions.

- Include any special invoicing instructions.

These are the instructions I used as a buyer. Ask your manager and other department leaders about any other important instructions. This is your show, these are your decisions. Once you have your instructions in place, stick to those rules; don't compromise on the needs of your organization. The rules should be maintained and managed, or errors may creep in. And when unwanted changes show up at the warehouse door, you are notified so you can push back on the mistakes. When mistakes occur, sales are lost, as inventories get out of joint. Create the standards in order to manage to the standards.

INVENTORY

Inventory can be your friend or worst enemy. Inventory issues can happen when you take your eye off the critical information including sell-through reports, open orders, and daily inventory levels. Watching the numbers every day can alert you and your team to alarming trends while they are still small. Today's inventory ages faster than ever before. Stores and e-commerce sites go out of business often because they have too much inventory. It becomes dated and worth way less than the sticker price. Look at your inventory reports daily, but also look at them over a week and then a month. Never wait for a product to rebound. When sales slow, begin the markdown process. You need to keep the goods moving, even if you are forced to give up some margin dollars. Sell-through is the key because overstocks can do great damage. One of the problems with any overstock is in not being able to buy the goods you need and can readily sell. You are stuck with poor good that are just not moving. Identify these slow movers and have a plan to move them out. Managing inventory while making money is what makes the organization hum.

PRICING

Buyers should believe every purchase is a winner. Some will be extraordinary, while others will land on the closeout rack. In regards to pricing, there are several items to consider:

- If you must follow supplier pricing policies, you already know the math from the start.

- Know that pricing policies refer only to advertising. In-store promotions and pricing is usually up to your organization.

- If you're planning to run in-store promotions, plan them out and work with your supplier for marketing collateral to support the promotion.

- You need a markdown strategy for when the bulk of the product slows down. As soon as that happens, put your sell-off program into action.

- If an initial presentation is slow to start, or worse, a failure, get your supplier to engage their support. They must bring help.

- Build a strategy calendar for every large introduction. Have discussions with the suppliers about how they can support your calendar. Markdowns should be a team sport. They should never rest solely with you. Suppliers have plans and programs for every situation baked into their strategies. But they tend to remain quiet except for their top accounts. Push them to share the markdown pain.

As you work out your initial retail pricing, be sure to include the issues of theft and damage, which can hit up to 3% of sales or more. Position these factors into your pricing schemes right through to that last markdown number. Pricing and the average gross margins are just as important as the choices you make. When I first became responsible for the overall management of business throughout my early career, I would get with management to create an all-inclusive markdown. This meant that if there was significant inventory, all goods were on promotion.

I later learned to become selective and would never again run a full-out sale on everything. Instead, I picked some items, but never the most sought-after 20%, which remained at full price. I learned I could sell off the poor items while still making top dollar on the best sellers.

Finally, what are acceptable gross margins? You probably have already been given those numbers by your manager or accounting team. If not, find out. Guessing, on acceptable margins is not a solid plan. In my industry, I always looked to achieve an average gross margin of 38%.

After markdowns and theft, that was a solid number. In a few roles, I received a bonus when the organization achieved a 36% gross margin for the fiscal year. It's also essential to have strict rules in place about personal or professional discounts. The sales team must be provided with rules of what they can and cannot do. Work with leadership on this critical policy. As you review daily sales, review all markdowns and the daily average margin. It's never OK to micromanage people, but you must micromanage every number important to your business.

BE PREPARED

Early in my career as a general manager, my belief was that impeccable planning would somehow create days without the stress other managers constantly faced. I would hire strong managers, secure the right products, and help create a winning advertising program. The goal was to hit sales targets while skipping over the standard managerial headaches. If I could remove potential problems from the start, I could remove the stress. Or so I thought.

It looked great on paper, but as you might guess, had little chance of succeeding. One year, in our largest sales month, we lost three strong location managers within 30 days. I had prepared for success, but never for the chaos that hit my desk. At that age, I was all work and numbers. But that was an amazing lesson that woke me up to the real world.

We live in a complex world where every employee has issues that can far outweigh their obligations at work. When people come to work, they bring all of themselves, including their personal lives and problems. That personal side cannot be kept on the other side of the door. Things happen. Everyone has issues that will affect their day. No matter how prepared you are, events will throw good plans out the window. Certainly, one thing you can do is to control the controllables. Work with your team to prepare to create a successful day. When the day takes a turn, the entire team should have plans B, C, and D for any number of problems that arise. Never believe every day will be perfect or that when employees have problems, they are pushing your buttons on purpose. Staff members get sick, show up late, or just outright quit. Do all you can to understand your business and work with your team to prepare for difficult situations.

Being a leader means more than always looking to charge forward. It's about knowing how to survive when the enemy is at the gate. Be flexible and don't panic. Remember the many fire drills you went through in school? Just as with that preparation, prepare for events and problems that will inevitably show up. Today, staffing is the daily question mark. Having an organization ready for whatever may come next is a positive way to keep engagement and people for the long term. People want to be around calm leaders. Panic serves no purpose.

No longer a coffee and donut event

You have a to-do list a mile long, that seems to grow every hour. One of the things you absolutely do not expect or want is the pop-in visit when a supplier "just happens" to be in your area and drops by with coffee and donuts. In my early years, sales reps seemed to have countless free hours to stop by and bother their largest accounts. The pop-in felt like a warm, kind gesture. In reality, it took people away from the work they had to get done that day.

The rep is there to talk business and find an order. They may want to remind you that you have inventory holes that require a fill-in order. Today, many reps are as busy as you. Business is good and many have little time to spare. Time wasters still exists however, and they appear in many different forms. One of the largest is your e-mail inbox. There are always fresh emails vying for your attention. It's important that your day is driven by your to-do list. Never allow someone else's problem to invade your day. Remain focused on those five or six items you prepared before the day began.

In addition to your to-do list, there will always be a few daily fires that will require your attention. Develop a discipline about your day. Be on purpose against those interruptions looking to take chunks of your time. Protect that time to get the best return and most value. Sure, accept the free coffee and donuts. Accept them, say thanks, and send the rep on their way.

The health of your supplier

In order to become a consistent, trusted partner, a supplier must have the financial health to do everything necessary to provide you with the products you need and the quantities you want. When a new supplier wants to become a partner, your role is to do the necessary due diligence and find out if they can supply their goods on time and fill reorders. It's especially important to not write orders with suppliers who push to ship quickly with tight payment terms. Even after suppliers have proven they can execute as requested, continue monitoring their health and status. Talk to other buyers from time to time and ask what they know. Paying attention to the financial health of your suppliers will help you keep your inventory where it needs to be. Never allow relationships to prevent you from doing your due diligence.

NEVER MARRY THE MERCHANDISE

This means you must act when inventory is backing up, while new orders continue to hit your stockroom doors. Success is about managing your inventory and being mindful of your sell-through every day. Waiting too long for a product to capture the eye of your customer is a timewaster. Customers quickly act or move on; they don't dawdle and wait around. This is not the time to have great patience that the overstock inventory will one day grow wings and sell through. Build a plan up front for every large buy. Create a program with a markdown schedule that takes you up to a 50% discount for the final units. Although the customer is always the big winner during any promotion, incentivize the salespeople. When you combine a sale price with a spiff (sales program incentive funds) program, you might be creating the fastest possible exit strategy. The best buyers work to average their margins through the course of the fiscal year. Never let the merchandise grow. Put this note on a Post-It on your laptop: I buy it to sell it!

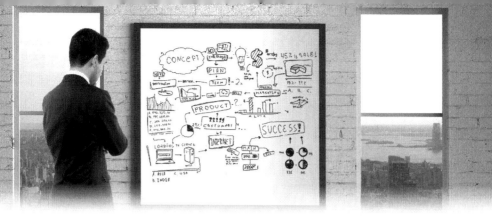

Relationships

"It's kind of fun to do the impossible."
Walt Disney

Creating a grand contact list takes time. It takes time, courage, and experience. As a buyer, building a strong set of relationships can help you keep merchandise flowing in tough times. Having a deep list of suppliers you call friends, as well as a deep list of competitors that will take your call can help enhance your success. Being able to gain favors from those suppliers you don't normally work with, is an added feather in your cap.

In good times, relationships are essential, in bad times they can be career-saving. Stay connected to each and every person on your list. Trade favors, do favors, and be cordial. There will be days you need help, so you need people who will be happy to take your call. Never say no. Never burn a bridge. Nurture your relationships. And be available to assist if you are able.

TRUST

The combination of being well-liked and trusted will make you the envy of your community. It can help you gain access to people and organizations some may not ever dream of during their caree Whether you're looking to connect to a prospective employer or great additions to your network, trust can open many doors. Take it away, and you have very little chance of moving beyond your current stage. Speaking of trust, suppliers and prospects should not gain access to your calendar if you don't trust them. There are far too many suppliers who want to work with your organization.

Working with people you cannot trust is a step into a dark room where anything can happen. There may be times you want to continue a program with a supplier, but you can't trust the representative. Talk to their sales management about your concerns. Chances are they won't make a change, which means you'll need to send the rep and the supplier on their way.

Along with being liked, you'll gain a reputation that has great value to your organization because you're trusted by those who get to work on your account. Work to continue to earn the trust of those in your supplier community, as well as those who may just be important to your future.

Your #1 Customer

When I became a buyer, I built a plan around providing the right product and best value to my customers. The plan became about satisfying every customer, every day. Being a part of the sporting goods industry, it was not hard to find people who had a passion for their sport and equipment. As the years rolled on, I learned more about buying and how to manage the role while serving the customer. I also took a deeper interest in the larger world of business, looking for new ideas about becoming successful in the role. I attended seminars, took courses, and visited competitors. I did everything I could to enhance my skills for the role and the industry.

I attended one seminar where I heard a message that changed my priorities. The speaker said that although we may be supporting hundreds or thousands of customers, our most important customer was our manager! That day I learned that before we worked to satisfy the wants and dreams of those customers walking through the door, we had to first satisfy our manager's expectations.

That changed how I thought about my job. From then on, I made certain that my manager was at the top of the list of people I needed to take care of. There will be days in your career where your manager doesn't understand your direction or methods. It's never good to pass over these concerns, believing they will blow away. It's important to communicate with your manager regularly. During times of disagreement or stress, you need to ramp up your communication. When the manager asks you to change plans or directions and you cannot sell your strategy, adjust and take the path recommended by your manager. Wearing down your boss will never end well. Your manager can be a great ally now and in the years to come.

Mentor

A mentor is someone who knows you. Although a mentor is not a paid part of your team, they are smart people, able and willing to help you for an extended period of time. They can help you choose the better fork in the road and make suggestions that might stir up new ideas. Mentors push and provide confidence. In many cases, they ask the questions that open up the answers for your next few moves. Mentors are with us to guide and support. They're not the answer man or woman who jump in and save the day. They assist in helping you build a better system for success. Because a mentor already knows you, they will be open, honest, and never afraid to say what is important in the moment. Think about a mentor when you need a special person providing important guidance to keep you on the right path.

Suppliers

You cannot do your job without your supplier network creating and distributing the goods you want to sell. It can be easy to spend much of your time and money with the major brands of your industry. Good idea right? They have the marketing, products, and consumer interest. It would make your preparation time so much easier. On the other hand, the largest brands generally offer the smallest margins, provide tighter terms, and push for larger orders in order to discourage challenger brands from grabbing shelf space. These suppliers continually tout their grand market share numbers, pushing you to not waste your time looking at other suppliers.

Every supplier is working to get your attention and win your business. No one tries to be number two or grab only small orders. Having worked for three challenger brands over the past several years, I know they research new ideas and new products all of the time. In fact, they had some of the most innovative products of the past decade within my industry.

The thing they lack is voice. They cannot be loud or speak often as they sorely lack marketing dollars and time. But they do stretch their competitive juices and take greater risks to get noticed. They need an opportunity and access to your calendar. Spend time every month looking at new brands and products that don't have the best names or largest marketing budgets. There is every chance you will find a few great new items that will drive interest, sales, and margin. Stretch beyond the top brands and look in new places. You will never be disappointed.

A WINNING SECRET

The office can be a comfortable place. It might be a reward for years spent learning and growing through the organization. It can also become a dangerous place because it's that place where information must come to you. That comfort in your personal space places you on a new level, with potentially a different attitude about the work.

The best buyers spend minimal time in their office. When they're done with their work, they get out to visit with the team, locations, and suppliers. They even just take walks to think new thoughts and mull over problems. They build their calendars to get the essential office work done then get themselves in front of as many people as possible every month.

No matter the information that comes to you, it's always through a filter, maybe several. When you look and listen, you will learn details that you'd never find any other way. I wish I had spent more time in the field. Spending more time with people rather than spreadsheets will result in more sales and improved consumer presentations. Ad hoc comments are very different from observation and conversation, so get deeper into the game and away from the stands as often as you can.

Your suppliers' best friend

In my early years, the relationships I had with many of my suppliers were, at best, cool. I was not an overly trusting person and I wanted to keep most everyone from the other side as far away as possible. Although we created some friendships, the relationships were separated by several miles. This was true until I came to a new organization with a very different kind of owner. He embraced his supplier network and treated every person the same, no matter the value of the brand to his stores. He held parties, took over entire restaurants, and gave awards while treating every person as a VIP partner. This was an amazing and essential lesson to learn in my 30s.

We ended up with great friendships that were far better than the usual supplier relationship. We were the first area account to receive the hot, new products, no matter how scarce the items were. We had a family of brand people fighting for us whenever there was an issue. To build better relationships with your supplier network, put them on equal footing. Treat their time with respect. Treat their teams with respect. There is every opportunity to win bigger when you treat your suppliers as members of your circle. When searching for a new supplier, look for ways to build a friendship, not just another vendor in your network. You will find yourself receiving more valuable perks and benefits. Every supplier has discretionary advantages. Being on their good side will enable more of the advantages to flow your way.

Invest in your network

There was a time during my career when I realized how valuable a network could be, and how I had done little to nurture it up to that time. In fact, I allowed my network to grow without my effort or my time. If I could go back to the age of 24, I would spend time every week looking into the professional leaders in my industry who could add value to my work. I would give anything to sit down with those smart industry leaders. Since then I have learned how to grow a network of value. I became proficient at communicating with those in my network.

After you have started to develop your professional network, you will want to learn how to support the members, ask for help, and nurture the relationships. A network is nothing like social media friends. Being part of a network means investing your time, skills, and support of members who will reach out from time to time.

There may be times you need help with a connection or a recommendation. No matter your age or current position, look for ways to step up and support members of the network. The value is in the giving, as well as the receiving of timely support. As with a savings account, there must be several deposits before you can extract a withdrawal, but there is value in the giving and receiving. With each interaction, you're building critical friendships that may not pay off for many years. There is no compensation for managing your network, but the support, direction, and wonderful friendships are priceless.

10-YEAR APPRECIATING ASSETS

This idea came to me when reading a book back in the '80s. I may have had a real focus on customer service, but reading about Carl Sewell, a Dallas Cadillac dealer, reset my entire notion of what customer service should be. Every sale had been about good service, the right product, a smile, and a credit card receipt. Certainly, as a consumer, I never felt that anything more than a transaction had taken place whenever I spent my money. Taking in this a-ha moment set a very new benchmark for how service should be conducted under my watch. This idea, centered on building a relationship with a 10-year plan in mind, provided me and my sales group with a new way to serve each customer. The strategy we implemented included these details:

- Create a specific, purposeful strategy.

- Build a long-term mindset from the first interaction with a person.

- Impart the same strategy with suppliers in order to achieve every advantage.

- Develop incentive programs that match the idea of building a long-term customer.
- It's essential to include every team member in this concept.
- Build a training program that will enable your team to see reasons to stay.
- Include product and pricing strategies into your 10-year program.
- Develop a people-friendly attitude for all transactions, including returns and damages.
- Bottom line: Create a daily program that is built from your customers' side of the sale.

When you treat your inside community as long term assets, the business will succeed and grow stronger over time. Viewing every customer as a long-term asset, whether they're spending money today or just browsing, absolutely creates a different point of view for the staff and your customers. Viewing people with a 10-year view will bring a new mindset to all. Loyalty is built one interaction at a time. Creating critical relationships will build tough muscles that will stand up when the economy suffers. At the same time, no single transaction is the ultimate one that matters most. Instead, it's the accumulation of goodwill over time. The positive interaction of today becomes the long term success for many tomorrows.

Communication

"A mistake is simply another way of doing things."
Katharine Graham

Whether negotiating with a supplier, training the team, or selling your manager on a large purchase, communication is your path to winning. To win means to communicate with excellence. Negotiating for the deal of the season means you're able to convey your message as few others can. Never stop working on your communication skills.

INFORMATION: THE MODERN CURRENCY

The buyer with the most current and accurate information will win many battles. Digging for and finding fresh, relevant detail is essential as you look to make the best decisions. So much of the information that hits your desk arrives from suppliers and their reps, so verify any information that comes to you. Although so much of the buying process is now automated, buying continues to require a sharp mind, a steady eye, and a degree of risk-taking.

Certainly, much of the basic information about brands, competitors and industry is just a click away. Reading industry websites will give you a solid picture of your world. You will find other important details through your most trusted industry allies and your own detective work. Hitting the road will also give you information not available through meetings in your office. Here are a few additional sources for valuable information:

- Invite supplier sales managers to visit with you. Spending time with important partner leaders will give you a wider snapshot of your industry.

- Schedule meals with industry connections, sales reps, sales managers and other leaders throughout the year. Conversations over meals will lead to important thoughts about products, competitors, and the industry.

- Build a schedule of consistent time out of the office. Visit with as many different connections, suppliers, and competitors as possible. The more people you visit, the clearer your competitive strategy should become.

- Have secret shoppers visit your locations as well as your competitors. Shop on your e-commerce site. Spend time in your customers' shoes to understand the process of being your customer.

ONE-ON-ONE

Your sale team is very busy. They have fewer people managing more things to do each day and it's a constant grind just to keep up. It can be tough to absorb important product details in a timely manner. Sending emails, product videos, copies of sales orders, and even full descriptions of new arrivals can all simply get lost in the craziness of the day. At one point I learned that simply throwing out detail, no matter its value, would rarely hit the intended targets.

The sales team needs to know the product information. They need to understand how to promote and sell the new goods. They must gain confidence quickly. Make time to work with individuals one on one. If your geography is too vast, and the sheer numbers prohibit this plan, get with the suppliers to create some great video content. Combine that with as many virtual calls as possible to drive home the product story.

Certainly, there is no substitute for time spent with individual team members. When your people are not educated and they lack confidence, sales will suffer. One-on-one is an important way to serve your team.

COMMUNICATION

One of the more important areas of your responsibility is communication: working with everyone critical to your success, sending them timely information for their role with each order. Building a communication system can help you develop consistent info for your program. A program that offers recognizable patterns can make each part of the work run well for each person. Consider how each purchase impacts the departments within the organization. You make the buy, and now the action begins.

You will need UPC codes then have the product detail entered into the system. The product has to be put onto the website complete with product images, descriptions, and pricing. Then the accounting and receiving teams must be provided the necessary detail.

Create a plan for communicating each new purchase throughout the organization. Leave plenty of time for training and answering questions about the new products. Communicating across all departments is how you will drive success for the organization.

IN THE LOOP

Things back up throughout the day including e-mails, calls, texts, and meetings. From the morning bell, you are immersed in your work. During the busiest times, it is easy to miss what else matters. One way to keep the focus is by keeping your manager in the know.

No leader likes surprises, and no manager wants to hear about serious issues after the fact. They will, however, also want to hear good news stories. Be proactive with your manager. Provide weekly updates and keep them in the loop on both the highs and lows of the week. Keeping your manager informed will help your most valuable relationship remain safe and open. Managers can become great members of your professional network and great resources for years to come.

SILENCE

After I had been a buyer for a few years, I discovered an idea that made the buying process work so much better. In fact, I began to call it a secret weapon. That idea was silence. You can use it in a number of ways. Whether it is being stoic during presentations, or not replying to a supplier right away, there is not much that will create more angst in a salesperson than silence. It was as if I had very little interest, whether that was true or not.

Over time, I used this tactic when it applied. It throws people off their game and creates speculation as to the quality of their offer. If you use it, you will most certainly create havoc and stress with the other side.

As with any major weapon, you want to use it sparingly. I found it an asset in gaining bigger advantages in a program. No is a reply salespeople are prepared to battle against, while silence confounds them. They don't know if you're busy or if you dislike the plan. They don't know their next move and may come back to you with a sweeter offer.

Everyone has a boss

Except for those people at the very top of the organizational chart, everyone has a boss. As you prepare to jump into negotiations for a new season or with a new supplier, discuss your plan with your manager and make sure they'll agree with your direction. No program can be a success if leadership isn't committed. Discuss the objectives and key points. There's no need to dive too deep into the minor pain points. You just want to keep the boss in the know, seek any advice, and ask for any feedback.

The one thing you never want to do is walk back a deal after you reached an agreement because someone up the chain has issues with it. On most days, business comes down to feelings and emotions in the moment. Although you go into every negotiation with a plan, there are people who may want to know why you settled where you did. Lay the groundwork upfront and bring your manager into the process early. In this case, the selling is on the other foot. You have to sell your plan to the boss. That person in turn, can sell it higher up the chain if necessary.

Buyers' Stew

"You miss 100% of the shots you don't take".
Wayne Gretzky

The following lessons could not find a place in other chapters, but they're vital to becoming a successful, well-rounded buyer, and are normally learned through experience and trial. These lessons, combined with on-the-job training will help you become a formidable buyer.

BUYER'S JOURNAL

Building a written history of the way you execute can be a useful resource as you grow in your role. Write down how you plan, make decisions, and the programs you sign off on. It takes discipline, which can pay great dividends. Buy a journal and use it. Each day, write a few lines about your work. When you are in negotiations with a new supplier or a new product season, detail the activity, your thoughts, and how you worked the process.

Your notes can include summaries of meetings, ideas for programs, or ideas about how to move forward. Add a summary at the end of each week. This journal can become your very own Masterclass of preparation, planning, and discovery.

Although I don't have one or two books filled with my secret buying formula, I have an office filled with legal pads, all filled with ideas and information, completed over several decades. I refer to them often. Creating a history of how you think and make decisions can become your secret sauce as you grow.

A THINKING SABBATICAL

In 1986, I discovered one of the important laws I was to follow for the rest of my career. This discovery showed me the many things I did not know about my work and my own shortcomings. I learned that becoming one of the top performers in a role would help me secure long-term employment, no matter the state of the economy. It also made me realize that being a top buyer would increase my income and future potential. Committing to this law changed everything.

Today, I suggest a thinking sabbatical to all of my mentees. The duration is an open choice, although I recommend a week. Move away from everything familiar: your office, the work, the house, and your routine to achieve this quiet. The sabbatical is to help you clarify issues of the past and resolve current situations, all while providing ideas for your next 12 months.

The important step is to clear your mind of everyday pain points that inhibit productive thinking. Your supplies can include a personal laptop, a stack of legal pads, and several good books.

This is not a vacation. It's a time to be alone with your thoughts and think about everything important to you, without the calls, texts, and interruptions. This is the time to think about your future. It is the time to write down every creative thought, every strange, crazy idea. This is your time to unwind, reset, and think about what life can really be for you in the next 12 months.

CONTINUOUS LEARNING

I made my first buy in 1979, and my buying career ended in 2010 when I moved into sales. In those early years, the world was already advancing beyond pencils, adding machines, and cash registers. In that first buying assignment, our organization was a pioneer: we installed a point-of-sale system. We were already traveling well above the speed limit.

As the years went by, technology infiltrated every phase of both the buying and sell-through ends of the transaction. Today, we work in a digital world with cloud storage. Certainly, Mr. J. C. Penney and Mr. Sears would have been amazed. No matter what you do or where you do it, the world is changing at warp speed. I was fortunate. I worked for an organization that brought in every bit of technology available to advance the operation, leaving competitors behind.

You need to use today's technology. And it's essential that your organization invests in it, not only to keep pace but to help you maintain your skills. Using the latest technology is part of a continuous learning process.

Learning is not just something people do while in school. It's now a life-long project, necessary just to keep pace with change and the younger generations, who were born into the idea of continuous improvement. No matter how comfortable you are with the tools of today, they can become obsolete rather quickly. Make a personal commitment to change and to keep learning.

Continuous learning helps you remain relevant, as well as grow new skills and opportunities. What I knew in 1979 or 1999 would not even get me an interview today, even though I was a successful buyer. Learning should include the hard and soft skills of general business.

CONTROL THE CONTROLLABLES

No matter how long your to-do list or deep your inbox, much of your day grows beyond your control. To understand the bigger picture, understand your place in your organization's success.

As the buyer, you are the person your team can count on for important product information. You need to understand your strengths and navigate around your weaknesses while spending the majority of your time where you will create the best results. You control your decisions and all of the preparation leading up to them.

Control what you can control by doing the necessary homework. It's your decision about what is purchased and what is not. You decide how the product presentation will work for your customers. Spend your time on what you can create and the direction you plan to move. You cannot control your competition, suppliers, or the economy. Tighten those things you can control. Sharpen every detail. Not every decision will turn out to be right. What is expected is that every decision you make is your best in the moment. Own the parts of the day you can control, and then negotiate the rest.

NEVER BELIEVE IN NEVER

I heard supplier after supplier say they would never add a category or even seemingly obvious items to their menu. No matter what many buyers thought, these vendors said "Absolutely not."

Those denials never stopped those in our buying fraternity to believe as we believed. Guess who eventually was right, most of the time? It is common sense that every organization must grow. That means they must add sales. New products grow a business. Wider menus and new categories can help any business grow as long as the items serve its offering. Combine this with new changes in management and you end up with new goods arriving at every turn. Managers drive ideas, as do competitors. So, never believe in never.

Base your decisions on what you can see, touch and purchase today. Take good notes and keep them filed away. There will be a day when "never" becomes "next season." You can always expect and count on change: constantly and forever.

YOU AS THE NEW BUYER

Do this exercise twice each year: Imagine that you are coming in to replace yourself as the buyer. It gives you the opportunity to look hard at those areas you might or should change. It also gives you a view into planning those things a new buyer might do to build a better business. Review your calendar, daily priorities, timewasters, untouched opportunities, quality of communication, and current inventory levels. There is no more honest review than that of the self. You can get an unfiltered review of your role and its execution, including both the hits and the misses. It can help you make the necessary changes you never had time to make. At some point, you may even bring a mentor in to help you. To be able to take a wide, critical look at your work, without fear is a gift. It's far better to do your own self-analysis than to have the leadership do it for you.

DEFINING YOUR STYLE

The more experience you gain in the buying role, the more your style will emerge. This style is really your strategy in how you do what you do. There are two distinct styles in when and how you choose products.

I have known some buyers who always want to have the new products first. They want to set a trend and have a leg up on their competition. They want the next purchase order to turn into the next great thing.

On the other side, there are buyers who take a wait-and-watch attitude. They have no interest in committing to a large buy, hoping their guess is a good one. They have no desire to set an early trend. They play the long game, waiting to see what works, and then buying based on trends and interest from customers.

I was a member of this last group. Having been burned too many times as a young buyer, I played the wait, watch, and then buy game. Because I was always with organizations of significant size, I would look to commit to some serious numbers once I felt a product was going to be a winner over time. Although many suppliers expect a significant commitment at the start of any new launch, if you do not feel confident in a new product, place a small test order, positioning the product in your top locations and a few in your weakest spots.

If you want to protect yourself, write a few future sales orders without purchase orders, in order to protect inventory. Once your test ends, decide how to move forward with your open orders. Every supplier expects all new introductions to become big winners, but that doesn't happen. Be sure you have a published rule that your orders must be backed by a purchase order number, in order to prevent supplier errors. You do not want truckloads of products not selling and taking up inventory dollars and space. There are two types of decision-makers here. Do you want it now, believing you are a buying savant, or are do you want to be certain this new introduction is a winner? It's your call to make.

HOLD THAT RESPONSE

Never, ever reply in anger. There are any number of good reasons for this. Yes, there are people who will not like you. There will be others who want to sell you products, break your rules, and push the envelope no matter the consequences. Still, you cannot lash out.

First, you are a professional, representing the many people of your organization. Next, although it's easy to punch back, it's smarter to understand the issue and solve it. Remember, the worst thing a supplier can do is to drop you from their lineup. That has far more impact than a fiery email. Even if you are a great communicator, there will be suppliers who do not hear or read. Others may simply ignore your instructions and ship when they prefer to ship, not you. There will be many days you may think, "Is anybody listening?" I spent several years being angry as a young buyer, so I feel qualified to offer these suggestions. When you become angry:

- Get out of your chair.
- Have a conversation with a friendly peer.
- Take a 15-minute walk.
- Go out for coffee or lunch.
- Blow off the situation for at least 30 minutes however you prefer.

There are a number of things you can do to calm yourself down and adjust the conversation in your head. The things you cannot do include:

- Returning a call when you're upset.
- Text anyone when you're angry.
- Have communications of any kind with anyone in the heat of the moment.

The goal is to allow enough time to pass. Communicating when you're angry, no matter the content, can only lead to escalation and further problems. Learn to hold your anger. Once you calm down, dig in to find out why others are angry and what can be done about it. If you are the angry one, allow a day to pass before investigating what happened. No matter what, you must be the smartest and calmest person in the room. Manage your anger in order to preserve relationships. Never reply with anger! There are no benefits.

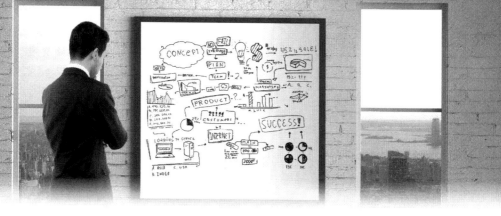

Marketing

"If you have everything under control, you're not moving fast enough."

Mario Andretti

Once the decisions are made and the buying is done, the buyer then sells their decision to everyone in the organization. Marketing is both telling and selling your ideas to move the plan forward. Work with people on the sales and marketing teams to create stories that can bring energy, excitement, and interest to the new products. You have as much to do with the successful sell-through as your initial decision to buy. There is much to do after the sales order is signed.

CREATING INTEREST

Advertising was the way to grab attention back when I began my first buying role. We were spending a lot of money in three areas: local television, radio, and print. Our boss knew that building a brand meant creating a consistent message over and over. There was no social media or even the internet, so blasting our message to a database was simply not an option. Telling a brand story today is called marketing; back then, it was just advertising.

The world has become a very noisy place. People wait for no one as they race through their day, focused on their needs and wants. Social media has certainly become a valuable asset. Grabbing attention and likes is the name of the game as every business stretches its creative juices to find that next idea to build love and loyalty. With the move to digital, suppliers can create interesting stories to attract consumers. As you develop conversations with suppliers about new product introductions or with prospects hoping for a green light desire shelf space, you need to know a few things about their marketing strategy.

Consider asking, what is their plan to promote the products they want you to buy. Where will they promote and how often? What assets will they make available to your team in order to create great stories on your web site? What images, videos and other assets will they share?

Marketing is about building energy, enthusiasm, and interest for new and different things. Although you're not a marketing guru, you're the person who drives the relationships with the suppliers. Include all of the right questions, then work with your team to create messaging that makes a difference. Stay connected to the product story long after the shelves are full.

PROCLAIM THE VALUE

Value is one word I heard over and over ever since the start of the pandemic. Certainly, it has been a part of the business world for a very long time. It seems to have taken on a much larger role during the most difficult period of our lifetimes. Value is that thing we expect with each purchase. It's what we want, but cannot see.

Whether we buy a product or service, value is the unstated expectation, no matter the money spent. For you, it's about communicating the value for the goods you purchased. Just as with a new blockbuster movie, your community must be made aware of the great new products coming soon. Work with your internal marketers as new decisions are made. Bringing the supplier into the conversation can possibly add a great number of interesting programs and promotions. The purchase is simply the beginning.

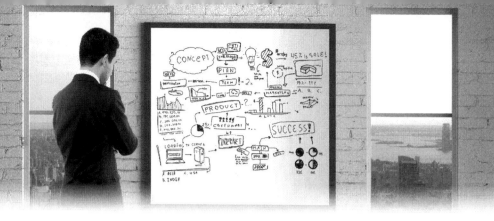

Attitude

> "The principle is competing against yourself. It's about self-improvement, about being better than you were the day before."
>
> Steve Young

You should always be thinking about sales success and helping the team drive new business. No matter if it's a good sales day or not, you carry the torch for the organization. Be positive about what will happen next. As the top cheerleader, you're out front, telling stories about the products and programs. No matter the current situation, you should be on high octane, working with the team, supporting and helping the business wherever you can. Being true but positive means being the best partner to leadership, the sales team, and everyone in the community.

First impressions

Creating an amazing first impression during the first 30 seconds of a meeting is an incredible skill. The first few seconds of an introduction will be the impression you have laid in cement with that person. Begin with a smile, an enthusiastic greeting, and a handshake (post-COVID), and give your full name. Next, listen to their full name. If it's not clear, ask again. There's nothing worse then missing the name of the person you just met, walking away, wondering what to do next? If you can treat each new person with the enthusiasm as if they are the most important person you'll ever meet, you'll gain many friends. Great first impressions are priceless. Practice this greeting with family and friends until it feels right. It must appear natural for you as if it is part of your DNA. It may feel intimidating, but meeting new people can make a difference in your career. You never know when the next person you meet might change your entire life's trajectory.

INTIMIDATED? ME?

You will have the opportunity to work with dozens of suppliers. Some may have already been part of your organization's lineup, others will be new. Some might be the largest in your industry. These may include the giant brands everyone covets. They expect to get their way in every situation. They tend to push, not persuade, buyers into position. Sometimes they may try to convince you the world will end if you don't buy according to their plan. Just remember, the person holding the purchase order holds control. There are times when these suppliers need to be reminded of that position.

There is never any reason to feel intimidated by any supplier. As long as you work your plan, you'll be fine. You're responsible for the purchasing, so you're in charge. Weak buyers act on the what-ifs about the supplier being right. Confident buyers will move as they should. In every case, you must own the room and be ready to take the lead. Never allow a person, or worse, a title to throw you off your plan. Be ready to listen, but never doubt yourself. The supplier meeting is about growing your organization, not theirs.

MISTAKES

Every buyer is an explorer, poking into new areas, searching for new discoveries. Testing new suppliers, product categories, and items can provide your organization with the knowledge of what might work beyond the standard menu. Since new discoveries move you away from the safe zone, you're apt to make some mistakes. It's alright; there's no need to stress. Building the business and becoming more effective means stretching beyond your comfort zone. As you move into new areas, you will make mistakes.

Buyers who work hard to avoid errors will fail in the long run. The best buyers know how to make money by taking risks. They combine the important core products, which drive sales but with lower margins, with new brands and a continual line of new products designed to recharge customers' energy. Buying is about making the best choices, but also about taking smart risks. Always favor your side with every decision. Make tests small and manageable. Just remember that if you're doing your job, you'll make mistakes. They're just part of the learning process and they're never fatal as long as you stick with the plan.

Rent your mistakes

No matter your role or level of experience, mistakes happen. Just as with the NFL quarterback who threw two first-half interceptions, they will still attack the defense throughout the second half, searching for cracks and opportunities because he reviewed his mistakes, spoke with his coaches, and learned how to adjust.

It's important that you study the buys that did not execute well. Once you have done your homework, move forward and continue doing your job. A bad buy is just that, it's not the end of the world. Never allow any mistake to shatter your confidence or hold you back.

The trick is to rent your mistakes. Accept them, learn from them, and then move on. Allow your skills and your many wins to push you past the hiccup. During my career, I made plenty of buying mistakes, but I quickly learned to recognize them and put together a promotional plan with the supplier to move them out quickly. And I learned from my mistakes for the future. Not once did a buying mistake slow me down. Good buyers produce solid results, not perfect results.

Success

"The people who are crazy enough to think they can change the world are the ones who do."

Steve Jobs.

Success for the organization means achieving sales and margin targets. It means selling through critical inventory and keeping poor buys to a minimum. That also goes for you. You're there to maximize each purchase, maintain proper inventory levels, and educate and inform your team and customers. There is no guessing about success. Every buyer knows at the end of the month, quarter, and year, how the report card will turn out. Success is also about enjoying your work. Try to laugh every day, and enjoy the work you do as well as the people in your community.

WORK TO LIVE, OR

I did not manage this area well during my buying career, so I hope you can learn from my mistakes. Whenever there is a discussion of work-life balance I snicker. Many so-called experts forget that no matter our personal expectations and how we propose to spend our time, there is another party in the conversation: our employer.

Many years ago I used the phrase, "the work never ends." Whether you end your day at 4:00 PM, or six hours later, your desk still has work on it that needs to be done. It shows up every day.

Once you realize the work never stops, you can look at how you want to manage your week. Some of us work to live and build a great life with our family and friends. Others live to work.

You need to decide. How do you want to manage your work life? That choice should be up to you. Decide how you will plan your work and then manage that plan. Don't allow the work to manage you. That is not a whiner's tale. Being purposeful in how you operate is essential to how you'll advance your career. It's your life and the decision should always belong to you. No matter your direction, it's your call. Just know that no one has ever spoken these words on their deathbed: "I wish I had spent more time at the office." Build a grand life beyond your desk.

COACH

Talent is an extraordinary gift. Exploiting your talents, you can create great success over time. It must be developed and honed over several years. In sports, every great player has had coaches, from youth sports all the way up through the professional ranks, coaches are there to guide, direct, and teach. Although being the best requires talent, talent alone will not win the race. Going at it alone is the same as a great football talent trying to play without any coaching. Depending on your role, your organization, and your growth plans, bringing in a coach to help you navigate through your career can be a unique opportunity.

Yes, coaches are an investment, but spending money to move up an extraordinary ladder can make sense. Even as a buyer, you have several areas to manage as you grow the business. Hiring a coach for a time can help you grow beyond the immediate future.

Although I never hired a coach, I had three mentors during my career. These individuals served as guides for me when I needed direction. They were experts when I had questions. If you can't make the investment to hire a coach, find a mentor. They are volunteers. They can help.

Coaches are experts at coaching, and they're paid to bring their specific skills, in order to help people move to the fast track. If you're interested in finding a coach, ask your suppliers, other buyers, and leaders within your community. Acquiring a coach or mentor will make a difference in how you plan, manage, and make decisions. Talent, no matter how great, requires nurturing and support to achieve extraordinary results.

ENJOY THE REWARDS

During my buying days, I served four great regional and national organizations. In that time, I received a great number of perks from the many suppliers: trips, special events, lots of mementos, and plenty of love. They made the long hours and extra work seem worth it over time. One mistake I made was in not taking advantage of several perks. I was always just "too busy." Not taking advantage of some of the gifts, especially the trips, was a big mistake. Industry trips are significant for networking with leaders and peers.

Please! Take the trips and perks that are offered. Anything that can put you in front of industry influencers has value beyond money. Do everything you can to say yes. These opportunities will not appear often, and then one day, they'll fade away. Spending time with unique and special people from your industry is truly a master class of networking.

ENJOY THE SHOW

I had the privilege of spending other people's money for three decades. It was an honor that I appreciated most days. Although I did understand the great gift of the job, there were other things I did not fully enjoy or appreciate along the way.

This lesson is my gift to you. Buying is a great job. It is a role where many look up to you as the smartest person in the room. While I was never that, I did the necessary homework to do it well. It may not feel like it today, but the time will fly by. Things may get missed. Enjoy your show.

Spend more time stepping back and admiring the people in your midst. I wish I had spent more time with many of the people I met. It would have been extra special to spend more time, have longer conversations, or even grab lunch or coffee outside the office. The money you earn gets spent and the gifts get used, but it's the memories that make the work all the more special. Take the extra time to get to know people. Enjoy the relationships you gain along the journey.

When you write your own book, you'll want to write about

the great people you meet throughout your career. Certainly, I spent time with some wonderful people. In thirty years, spending lots of money, that's inevitable. My regret? I should have slowed down and gotten to know people far better. I should have asked more questions of more people. Cherish your gift, and enjoy the show. They are the memories you will look back on and remember with a smile.

Summary

> "If you love your work, if you enjoy it, you're already a success."
>
> Jack Canfield.

In my mind, there can be no better way to earn a living than being a buyer. The role holds great sway. People treat the buyer with extraordinary care and attention. Every day is new, with different challenges and different opportunities.

At the same time, it's a job. There are expectations coming at you from several directions. Because there are expectations, the role requires great thought, planning, and deliberation.

One takeaway I want to reinforce here is the trial. When in doubt about a new product line, put together a test order. Assemble your supplier, inside team, and other local assets necessary to give this test 100%. If it doesn't work, move on. Trials are valuable whenever doubt creeps in.

The next takeaway is that of trust. There are any number of times you'll want to reach out and ask for advice from someone in your circle. Build a tight circle of select advocates to call on when you need help. Trust is the essential connector.

Another takeaway is to get out of the office. No doubt it's a comfort zone where you control the space. Moving out into the world opens you up to connecting with and recognizing team members. This is a great opportunity to mentor, teach, and thank your team for all they do. By making the time to visit your locations, you learn about teams, the product presentation, and the reasons for the results on those daily sales reports. Another benefit is seeing the competition up close for yourself to understand the differences in operations. Overall, traveling to these locations on a regular basis will open your eyes to things you can never learn from behind your desk.

The next takeaway is to borrow. There are great ideas everywhere. Some are located with your competitors, but many are in other industries that can be used in your business. Many great business leaders borrowed from other companies in order to test or tweak ideas that might have a variety of uses. As you visit your competition, use your phone to jot down notes on things you like. The same goes for different industries outside your own. The first step is to borrow. The next is to transform the idea to fit into your box. Develop trials to work out the possibilities. That next winning idea might be across the country or the store down the street. Open your eyes to what you might see and open your mind to what you can recreate.

Recognition is a most valuable takeaway. It shows strong leadership when you recognize team members, corporate staff, and those suppliers who enable you to move the business forward. Thanking people for their efforts is never just a glancing acknowledgment. It may take only a minute or two to do it, but that recognition can last a long time. Whether verbal or in a thank you note, showing someone you appreciate them is an act of grand leadership.

Next, consider your supplier network. A business cannot operate without the items necessary to create and service customers. Smart buyers should treat their suppliers as partners. Their shelves remain empty until a supplier executes an order. Glitches do occur, but you should never throw rocks at your supplier. They're not accepting your orders with the hopes that something will go wrong; they're trying hard to succeed. Treat them well in return and watch what can happen.

Finally, buying today is now all about learning. Every major role is now attached to acquiring new major role that is not attached to acquiring new knowledge and skills. There are daily opportunities to build relationships, but you also need time to seek out new information on software, communication, apps, and other assets. You can no longer remain static, stand pat, or remain the same executive you were yesterday. The best place to be is where new ideas are available. These are the places to drive new trials and discoveries for you and your organization. Those who own new skills and understand how to treat others will create better businesses in the future. Enjoy the journey. Boring work days are a thing of the past.

Million Dollar Takeaways

Introduction

> "Ideas are easy. Execution is everything. It takes a team to win."
>
> John Doerr.

There are people in every industry that stand out, that do more, give more and earn much more. There are great examples of men and women who through trial and error, through sheer grit and determination, learn to thrive, no matter the weather or the economy. They have learned how to get it done in the best of times and then in those times when the competition just doesn't want to fight the battle. The men and women in this category relish the climb.

During the early years of my career, I realized that watching and mimicking the winners inside my world would give me a leg up in my organization, my world, and my industry. From that early start, I have continued to seek out the brightest stars. In this section, I present men and women who have, over time, developed the skills, the persistence, and the ability to execute. This section: The Million Dollar Takeaways, provides lessons from people who simply understand how to succeed. If you read and digest only this section, this book will be an amazing investment for you today and for many years to come.

Marc Feocco

As a category manager for a major brand, Marc has been in sales and sales management for decades. He totally understands his world, his organization, and the customers he serves. He has built a successful career due to his commitment to always doing the right thing, as it pertains to his customer. Here are Marc's thoughts:

Selling rules

- Look for the need.
- Also look for the wants of each client.
- Fill the need and then look to expand the want.
- Learn the communication style of each customer.
- Get an early start to the day.
- Work hard to stay current with all of your communications.

Marc's thoughts on buyers

- Marc assumes they know their business.
- Better buyers are prepared and they buy to the opportunity.
- They know their customers.
- They know their numbers.
- They are always looking to be creative.

Thoughts on COVID

- It has changed the world of selling.
- It has also changed the way business gets done.
- It has made it necessary for reps to prepare presentations beyond face-to-face meetings.
- Post-COVID is the time when the trusted supplier become the trusted business advisor.

Wish I knew at 22

- Learn to become a much better listener.

Marc's career takeaways

- Treat every client as a 25-year business partner.
- Do what you say you are going to do.

Susan Shade

These are the grand lessons. The lessons learned over time. They include the skills executed day after day for decades, first to make a living and then to create a great life. The value of these professionals is extraordinary. The value of their lessons, priceless!

Susan is a long-time successful sales executive. She has been in the retail and apparel industries throughout most of her career. She is a leader, a mentor, and a trusted friend to many in her industry.

Susan's rules for sales success

- Understand the important data and the numbers.

- Come into each day prepared.

- Talk about what your buyers believe, then mold it to gain a mutual understanding.

- Step back to look at the list of priorities on a regular basis.

- Always deal with customers' issues before anything else.

What I wish I knew at 22

- To know that business is about partnership.

- To be and to remain humble.

- That at 22, no one expects you to know it all.

Sales after COVID

- Some customers will accept a virtual sales presentation.
- Buyers will continue to rethink their strategy.
- The price of admission for new brands will be higher.
- Sales professionals must be more tech-savvy.

Regaining a lost account

- Work to rebuild trust.
- Ask the buyer what it will take to earn back the account.
- Know it may take more than your organization is willing to give.
- Understand there are other times it may take less than you think.

Susan's Platinum Rule

- Always do what you say you are going to do.

Mary Schell

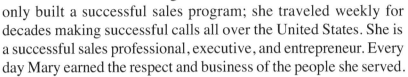

A long-time sales executive. Mary bought a company that was in dire need of saving. She not only built a successful sales program; she traveled weekly for decades making successful calls all over the United States. She is a successful sales professional, executive, and entrepreneur. Every day Mary earned the respect and business of the people she served.

Mary's rules for success:

- The first meeting with a buyer is never a dog & pony show. It is a meeting to learn.
- Mary looks to find out where the customer's focus is.
- Is there a fit for her product? If yes, what is that fit?
- She will dig to find the buyer's end needs.

Mary's secret sauce:

- She has a passion for her customers, not her products.
- Mary helps her customers build a revenue stream.
- Mary works to make her customers successful.

Wish I knew at 22:

- Find a strong, experienced mentor.

Great buyers:

- Listen.
- Educate themselves.
- Educate the sales rep and the supplier, too.

Winning back a lost customer:

- Ask for a 15-minute face-to-face meeting.
- Mary offers an apology: 4 minutes.
- Mary explains what happened: 4 minutes.
- Mary commits to a successful to-do list going forward: 11 minutes.

Final thought:

- Build enough of a financial basket to stay on the road, to build your future.

Luan Pham

Luan has been a successful sales and marketing professional for decades. He has not only succeeded; he has succeeded in a number of divergent industries. Luan understands his worth and the worth of every one of his customers. If information is the golden ticket, Luan has an endless global Fastpass. With Luan, it is all about information and then execution.

Luan's rules for success:

- Provide incredible benefits.
- Never look at a sale only as a single transaction.
- View the account relationship as a long-term program of discovery.
- Help customers locate new business.
- Look past what is right in front of you.
- Share ideas with customers, helping to grow relationships.
- Think about the human side; realize there is another person on the other side of the desk.

Luan's success standards:

- He looks for opportunities to help his customers.
- He has courtesy and respect for every customer and prospect.
- Luan realizes that every account is a unique riddle that he will untangle.
- He goes into each day accepting it will bring new challenges.

- With Luan it is people first. He is constantly checking in on the people in his community.

Wish I knew at 22:

- Have passion for what you do.
- To have grit.
- To build a relentless pursuit towards achievement.
- Listen to your heart.
- Do not be afraid.
- Commit to the work.
- Prepare for future success.

Luan's Secret:

- Selling is not a race against the other person.

Luan's Secret Sauce:

- I reach for the stars every day.

Bill Heubach

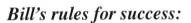

Bill has been an executive in the apparel industry for much of his career. In addition to being high on the org chart within his organization, Bill is a full-time sales professional, serving accounts all over the United States. Bill is well-liked and respected by his accounts. He really doesn't have customers, just an industry filled with friends. Bill manages his business for his customers.

Bill's rules for success:

- Listen intently to your customers.
- Know your buyers and their business.
- Enjoy what you do for a living.
- Always be sincere and humble.
- Make the most of the face-to-face time with your accounts.
- Never spend time selling products your buyers do not want.
- Understand what your customer is thinking.
- Always put the needs of customers first.

Wish I knew at 22:

- To take the work seriously.
- Take advantage of every opportunity given.
- Be early to every sales call.
- Value your customers' time.

Lessons from tough times:

- Talk to business leaders who have lived and survived through tough times.

 Look at your profession and your work in the long term.

- Bill believes that success is built on relationships, not price.

Bill's other rules:

- Be organized.
- Plan out the specifics of every meeting.
- Develop a strong work ethic.
- Plan your calendar 3-4 weeks out.

Bill's secret sauce:

- He always puts his customers' needs in front of his own.

Bill Sweet

Bill is a career sales professional, always playing at the top of his game. He has an amazing record of achievement and the honors to match. Bill has spent his career in the sporting goods industry, covering the Midwest. He knows and respects his customers and they return the honor. He knows his industry, product, and and amazing lineup of customers. Bill wins, no matter the economy because he has persistence and grit — special gifts we all can use more of today.

Bill's rules for success:

- Bill does the essential research before an account meeting.
- He is very well organized.
- He plans out his calendar weeks in advance.
- Bill remains open to new ideas and new products.
- He checks his voicemail in the early morning and throughout the day.
- Bill also checks his texts and e-mails prior to starting his day.

Bill's standard:

- Never give false information.

His thoughts on his profession:

- Building relationships is and will always be a critical part of his sales success plan.
- Every sales professional must be tech-savvy.

Bill's homework:

- After a meeting with an account, Bill looks at what went well and not so well.
- Bill constantly provides feedback to his suppliers.
- He provides ideas to his suppliers.

Wish I knew at 22:

- Get up early every day.
- Answer every phone call.

Bill's secret sauce:

- Bill's mantra: Return all calls and e-mails in a timely fashion, no matter the situation. Always be honest and most times things will work out.

Will Carswell

A long-time seasoned sales executive in the sporting goods industry, Will understands both the important account detail and the essential back-of-the-house information. Will has been a successful sales professional, sales manager, and company executive. He has great care and empathy for his sales reps and customers. He is analytical in his approach and long-term in his planning. Will constantly challenges himself to be better at the goals set for him by the organization.

Will's rules for success:

- Will prepares for his day the evening before.
- He reviews his calendar every morning.
- He also reads unread texts and e-mails early.
- He asks lots of questions in his sales meetings with customers.
- He always puts the interest of his customers first.
- He looks to be genuine every day.

Will's sales tools:

- His #1 sales tool is his paper notebook. He writes everything down.
- His other tools include his amazing network of industry people.
- His MacBook.
- The many mobile Apps he has downloaded.
- His list of personal contacts.

Thoughts on buyers:

- The best buyers are self-aware.
- The best buyers understand the needs of their business.

Will's rule:

- To prioritize the needs of the business each and every day.

Eddie Drye

Eddie has been a long-time success in more than one industry. Eddie is relentless in his pursuit of building true friendships with his customers. If you are not a friend of Eddie Drye, it is certainly not his fault. He has been a sales professional, a sales trainer, and is now an executive. Working with his tank always at full, Eddie continues to perfect his team and his presentation.

Eddie's rules for success:

- Success lies in asking questions, not in a long pitch.
- Eddie spends almost 90% of the appointment time asking questions.
- He likes to create a trial close a third of the way into the presentation.
- He believes too many reps take the long path to yes.

Eddie's secret sauce:

- It is vital to gain trust early in a relationship.
- He views selling like hiring: it takes time, homework, and preparation.
- He suggests throwing an odd question at the buyer, getting the buyer to think differently.

The best buyers:

- Are great listeners.
- They approach every meeting with a plan.
- The best buyers are humble.

Additional success thoughts:

- Offer your buyer a new tactic or strategy. Something that may be a new idea.

- Things change quickly, and the sales pitch requires updates.

- Dig into what your buyer needs before you make your pitch.

- Education is the least used tool in selling.

- It's critical to educate your buyer early, on your brand and product categories.

- A long-range sales plan of 12-24 months will bring greater sales success.

Bob Duncan

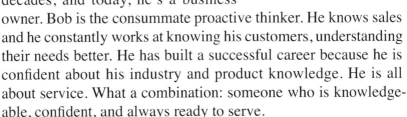

Bob is all about the sales process. He has been selling for decades, and today, he's a business owner. Bob is the consummate proactive thinker. He knows sales and he constantly works at knowing his customers, understanding their needs better. He has built a successful career because he is confident about his industry and product knowledge. He is all about service. What a combination: someone who is knowledgeable, confident, and always ready to serve.

Bob's rules for selling:

- Ask lots of questions.
- Know what the customer wants before you move toward a sale.
- Believe in yourself.
- Most buyers say no because they simply do not know enough.

Wish I knew at 22:

- Study harder.
- Put family first.

Post-COVID world:

- Make the pitch fast and friendly. We're in a microwave world; attention spans are shrinking.
- Get your key idea across in seconds.
- Do not take people out of the process.

Bob's modern-day concern, especially for small business:

- Who is going to survive the internet?

Kevin McClellan

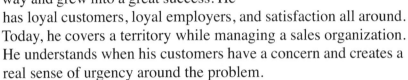

Kevin McLellan sees the world clearly from three feet as well as from 3,000. He came up the long way and grew into a great success. He has loyal customers, loyal employers, and satisfaction all around. Today, he covers a territory while managing a sales organization. He understands when his customers have a concern and creates a real sense of urgency around the problem.

Kevin's rules for selling:

- Set expectations for every sales call.
- Know your product cold.
- Set expectations with his buyer.
- Listen hard.
- Develop great fundamentals to use on every sales call.
- Treat every customer dollar as if it is your own.

Wish I knew at 22:

- Never beat yourself up.
- Continue to tell yourself to stay true to who you are.
- Enjoy the journey.

Valuable sales tool:

- The Franklin Covey Planner. It is old school, and it helps Kevin plan his week.
- Kevin writes everything down and leaves nothing to chance.

The best buyers:

- Are strong communicators.
- Ask the right questions.
- Look to achieve a partnership.
- Trust the rep to do their job well.

Kevin's words to live by:

- Be honest.
- Treat people as they want to be treated.
- Do what you say you are going to do.

Steve Brady

Steve is a real Renaissance man. He has succeeded in several industries, every industry he decided to tackle. In time, he analyzed the need and attacked the opportunity with a down-home, personal attitude that makes people feel as if they are working alongside a friend. Steve has recently achieved amazing success in another new industry, where likability, attention to detail, and the human touch all play a part. It is obvious that any venture Steve approaches, he'll find the need, fill it and succeed.

Steve's rules for success in selling:

- Know the market.
- Know your numbers cold.
- Be unique: do not look and sound like your competition.
- Use your network, as well as all available industry resources.
- Listen intensely.
- He works hard to be liked and to be trusted.
- He cares about every customer
- Steve creates a connection with his customers, assuring them he will their best interest at heart.

Steve's routine for success:

- Steve takes a walk every day.
- His goal is to have 20 conversations every day.
- He has an intense focus on follow-up.
- He uses time blocking as an important part of his success tool kit.

Wish I knew at 22:

- Never stop building relationships.
- There is no success secret.
- To focus on the things you do well.

Steve's secret sauce:

- He builds relationships that last.
- He works very hard to be a trusted resource.
- Steve shows genuine interest in his customers.

The future of sales:

- The experience of face-to-face selling will continue to be important.
- The personal touch will be critical.
- Listening will always be a crucial part of the success formula.
- It will be important to relearn how to work smarter as the world changes.

Steve's takeaway:

- Referrals are critical. There is nothing more powerful than one buyer recommending you to another buyer.

Scott Smith

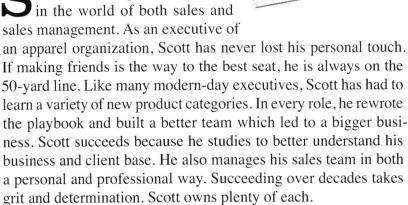

Scott is a long-time veteran in the world of both sales and sales management. As an executive of an apparel organization, Scott has never lost his personal touch. If making friends is the way to the best seat, he is always on the 50-yard line. Like many modern-day executives, Scott has had to learn a variety of new product categories. In every role, he rewrote the playbook and built a better team which led to a bigger business. Scott succeeds because he studies to better understand his business and client base. He also manages his sales team in both a personal and professional way. Succeeding over decades takes grit and determination. Scott owns plenty of each.

Scott's rules for success:

- Simplify the transaction for each customer.
- Make every new account set-up as seamless as possible.
- Learn about your customers' business.
- Return customer calls the same day.
- Build follow-up plans that place a sense of urgency at the core.
- Your sales team must know the product story inside out.

Scott's ideas for this new world of selling:

- Move faster towards new technology.
- Every independent sales professional should create their own website.
- Scott never wants a cold meeting with a prospect.
- Scott suggests creating video presentations for customers.

- Scott believes the future will be about new ideas and yet undiscovered technologies.

Other suggestions on selling success:

- Study your mistakes to learn where the misses occurred.
- Play the role of partner to your customer.
- Develop more of a long-term success strategy. Create a flexible 3-6 month plan.
- Understand that a No is not personal.
- Be persistent.

Scott's morning routine:

- Follow up on all open items.
- Review the actions and results of the previous day.

Scott's success takeaway:

- There is extraordinary value in being a good listener.

Chuck Thiry

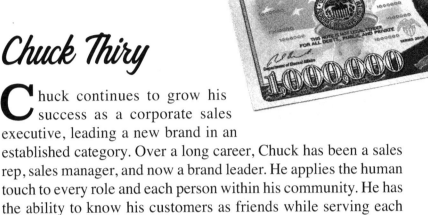

Chuck continues to grow his success as a corporate sales executive, leading a new brand in an established category. Over a long career, Chuck has been a sales rep, sales manager, and now a brand leader. He applies the human touch to every role and each person within his community. He has the ability to know his customers as friends while serving each as if they were his only client. He knows how to develop a sales team in the way championship coaches create winning teams. He works closely with both the individual and their abilities. As an experienced leader, he continues to attack the challenges of this new world of work.

Chuck's rules for success:

- There is no real success secret. Successful salespeople are honest and hard-working.
- Look to provide simple answers to customers.
- Sales is a total numbers game.
- Salespeople who make the most sales calls win.
- It is essential to earn the trust of every customer.
- Chuck believes it is not essential to love all customers, as some are hard to love.
- Learn what makes your toughest customers tick. Many times they are your best customers.

Chuck's thoughts on sales rep compensation:

- Sales rep compensation should be tied to company profitability where possible.
- Every team member should be invested in the continued

success of the enterprise.

Chuck's thoughts on buyers:

- Service can improve through strong relationships.
- It is easier to attract more business using honey rather than demands.

Chuck's thoughts on the future of sales:

- Face-to-face meetings will continue to be important.
- Creating and sustaining relationships will be critical for future success.

Matt Zarilla

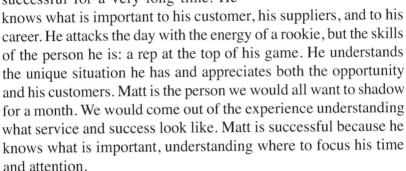

Matt is an independent sales professional. He has been successful for a very long time. He knows what is important to his customer, his suppliers, and to his career. He attacks the day with the energy of a rookie, but the skills of the person he is: a rep at the top of his game. He understands the unique situation he has and appreciates both the opportunity and his customers. Matt is the person we would all want to shadow for a month. We would come out of the experience understanding what service and success look like. Matt is successful because he knows what is important, understanding where to focus his time and attention.

Matt's rules for success:

- Sell units. Don't worry about dollars within a transaction.
- Selling is the easy part. Getting the appointment is the challenge.
- Within each presentation, read the body language and potential buying signals of each customer and prospect.
- Come into every presentation with a deep knowledge of your products and programs.
- Fight for your accounts. When there is a dispute, look for resolution, never blame.
- Relationships are critical to success in sales and in building personal rewards.

What the best reps do:

- They listen well.
- They are proactive in their approach to a customer

or prospect.
- They always show up.
- They outhustle the competition.

Matt's thoughts on the profession of sales:
- Sales is about convincing people to change.
- It is the freedom to build income without limits.
- It is a unique opportunity, a game-changer for those who recognize it in that way.

Matt's secret sauce:
- He is consistent.
- He is honest with customers and suppliers.
- He has developed strong communication skills.
- He answers every phone call.
- He responds ASAP to every customer request.

Matt's thoughts on the future of sales:
- There will be sales professionals selling and serving 50 years from today.
- The field will be different. The need to build relationships, service in a timely way, and provide consistent follow-up will remain important parts of the success playbook.

Jackie Kirkwood

Jackie has been successful as a retailer, buyer, sales rep, and corporate sales executive. She has great skills working with customers while always taking care of her team. Jackie has a unique discipline, understanding the world from both sides of the desk. She continues to succeed, serving world-class and industry-leading brands. Her secret sauce is her ability to understand the needs of the account. She has done that with great focus over several decades. She is that leader that young sales professionals would be lucky to have as their manager.

Jackie's rules for sales success:

- Jackie looks to eliminate the sense of process from the presentation.
- Jackie looks always to create a conversation.
- She works to build rapport with the customer.
- Jackie works also to take away any thoughts of failure.

Jackie's secret sauce:

- It is important to work for the right organization.
- She focuses on the long term, not only the day ahead.
- Jackie works to help her team take the steps to move down the right path.
- She doesn't overly concern herself with the money piece.

Wish I knew at 22:

- Be a bigger sponge.
- Be sure to enjoy the ride.

What do great buyers do:

- They are great listeners.
- They are focused observers.
- They develop relationships with their sales representatives.

Changes due to COVID:

- COVID has forever changed face-to-face meetings.
- The process of the sales presentation will be different and varied across the account list.

Jackie's key takeaway:

- Remember that sales is the lifeblood of the business!

Tom Schmidt

Tom is a seasoned professional with experience in several industries. He began his career in retail, eventually moving to the B-to-B side of sales. Tom is a disciplined rep with a sincere focus on doing the right thing for his customer. He understands that learning and growing is the equivalent of giving himself a raise. As the sales profession changes, Tom knows he must continue to move in new directions. He has been successful in more than one industry because his focus is on his customer, not his product.

Tom's rules for success:

- Know both your product and the competition far better than your customer does.
- Preparation is key.
- It is essential to know technology.
- Tom knows he must remain agile in the face of change.
- Tom walks into his appointment as the expert in the room.
- Tom knows it is important not only to know your product but its backstory.
- It is important to get to the bottom line with your customer.
- Tom challenges the buyer to move to a positive decision.
- Tom asks lots of questions during the sales call.
- Travel to the business. Focus on seeing the top accounts first.
- Tom focuses too on the needs of his organization.

- Tom continues to work on getting access to prospects.

Wish I knew at 22:

- Learn where to travel.
- Know what to focus on.
- Product knowledge is critical.
- Know your product story inside and out.
- Understand that you are the resource for the customer.

Tom's secret sauce:

- He works less on building relationships, more on cultivating sales.
- Tom works to create a bit of positive tension during the presentation.
- Tom is direct in asking questions of his customers.
- Tom works to move customers beyond their comfort zone.

Tom's plan for earning back a lost account:

- Tom writes a letter of apology to all involved.
- Leaving ample time, Tom then looks to restart a conversation.
- He takes baby steps in looking to earn a face-to-face meeting.
- He asks if everyone can simply move on from the mistake.

Tom's key takeaway:

- The 80/20 rule is a large part of success in sales. Overserve your top 20%.

Jeff Lienhart

Jeff understands that relationships not only create business opportunities, they enhance the business over the long term. Jeff is a long-time sales leader, manager, and executive. He has been with some of the largest brands in the sports world. It's the effort, the hard work, and the persistence over time that has helped Jeff create a successful career. As a brand leader, Jeff focuses on what makes the engine go: the product, people, story, and the way his team serves customers. No matter the logo on his shirt, Jeff always works with the same vigor and passion for people, customers, and building successful organizations.

Jeff's rules for sales success:

- Establish priorities.
- Come into every customer situation with an open mind.
- There must be mutual trust.
- It is important to take quiet time to think.
- Look beyond the efforts of just this one day.
- The best situation is when the customer feels as if they are not being sold.
- Victories cannot be one-sided.
- The status quo is your enemy.
- There is always a better way.

Wish I knew at 22:

- Be organized.
- Be transparent.

- Set personal expectations.
- Acquire a mentor.
- Mistakes happen when you just try to wing it.

Jeff's thoughts on COVID:

- Virtual presentations and webinars are here to stay.
- COVID created the immediate need for all to learn new skills while going digital.
- COVID exposed new business opportunities.

Jeff's thoughts on the future of sales:

- The profession will become more sophisticated.
- Salespeople will need to become savvier.
- Relationships will continue to be important.
- The changes that occurred during COVID will remain.

Jeff's key takeaway:

- Do what you say you are going to do.

Daniel Botero

Daniel is the one successful sales professional in this book from a different generation. He sees the world from a very different set of eyes. He is a true risk taker, and he is a proactive success as a young entrepreneur. Daniel was a sales leader with a Fortune 500 company with a large territory. As a sales leader, he was proactive and successful. However, he had the desire to do his own thing. Although decades younger than many entrepreneurs, Daniel has been a real inspiration to me over the past few years. He is always learning and looking for a simpler way to get things done. There is no doubt Daniel will continue to grow his business while supporting others.

Daniel's rules for sales success:

- Each transaction must be a win-win.
- Change up priorities every 90 days.
- Understand each client and their specific needs.
- Reset your goals for the next: 1/2/3 years.
- Once a year, align your business goals to that of the organization.

Daniel's take on the future of sales:

- Consultative selling is becoming ever more important.
- The best sales professionals are truly all-powerful and vital to business success.
- Technology is making business more effective and efficient.
- The higher the price sticker, the more face-to-face time is critical.

- AI is now supporting part of the sales process for large brands.

Daniel's sales tools:
- His personal brand standards are critical.
- Linkedin is an important part of Daniel's success.
- Daniel writes down the details of every win. He will go back and read and reread each winning entry to recall the sensation.

Daniel's key takeaway:
- There is a well-guarded wall between the buyer and seller that must come down.

Shawn Harris

Shawn has been a hero of buyers for many years and has served in more than one industry. He goes out of his way to more than satisfy the customer. He has taken his deep service mindset and created great standards with a new, very different set of customers. He is genuine and authentic. He comes into his day with a plan for the customer. As a successful sales pro, Shawn continues to search for ways to create more sales and success for his customers and does it with tenacity and truth. Shawn has been a favorite rep of mine for a long time.

Shawn's rules for success:

- Executes his service story as if he is working for the customer.
- Search for the customer's need and satisfies that need.
- Do great preparation prior to any sales meeting.
- Review all account data before any meeting.
- Be persistent.
- Write out sales plans for the week on Sunday night.
- Push through the pain of rejection.

Wish I knew at 22:

- Success happens slowly, brick by brick.
- Buyers do things on their time.
- Management has expectations.
- It is important to move in baby steps at the start of a new relationship.

- Play the long game. Be patient.

What he wants to do better:
- Improve his listening skills.

What great buyers do well:
- They communicate well.
- They do not sugarcoat their feelings.
- They trust and they want to be trusted.

Where is the sales profession headed:
- The profession is moving to consultative selling.
- There will be more key account reps and fewer boots on the ground.
- Industries vary, change will come differently to each.
- Key account reps are doing more of the planning and strategizing.

Shawn's key takeaway:
- Proper preparation and review is critical for success.

Lou Ramos

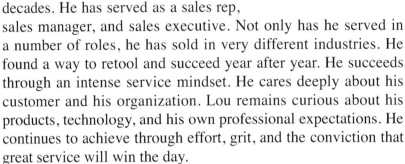

Lou has been a success in sales and sales management for decades. He has served as a sales rep, sales manager, and sales executive. Not only has he served in a number of roles, he has sold in very different industries. He found a way to retool and succeed year after year. He succeeds through an intense service mindset. He cares deeply about his customer and his organization. Lou remains curious about his products, technology, and his own professional expectations. He continues to achieve through effort, grit, and the conviction that great service will win the day.

Lou's rules for success:

- Be totally prepared.
- Have the account data ready for every meeting.
- Know what the account has purchased in the past.
- Develop and build relationships.
- Work to leave something of yourself or your organization with the customer or prospect.

Wish I knew at 22:

- If sales is about only the money, get out of the profession and find another industry.
- To actively engage in the work of your organization.
- It is important to weave yourself into the fabric of your organization.

Lou's important skills:

- His ability to tell stories.

- His ability to communicate well, both verbally and in writing.
- He gets up early every day.
- Lou learned it is important to confirm appointments a day before.
- He prepares his day the night before.

Overcoming tough times:
- Work to have high energy for every sales appointment.
- Focus on the now. Do not think about the results of the past.
- Accept both highs and lows with the same attitude.
- With every new month beginning at zero, it is the opportunity to create new success.

What great buyers do:
- They're willing to take risks.
- They look to include the sales professional and supplier in their process.
- They look to create partnerships with their suppliers.

Lou's rule:
- My phone is never on vacation.

Dawn Hulett

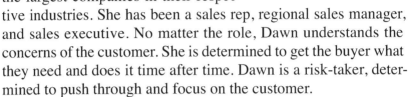

Another successful sales veteran, Dawn has worked for some of the largest companies in their respective industries. She has been a sales rep, regional sales manager, and sales executive. No matter the role, Dawn understands the concerns of the customer. She is determined to get the buyer what they need and does it time after time. Dawn is a risk-taker, determined to push through and focus on the customer.

Dawn's rules for success:

- Focus always on the account, not on achieving specific numbers.
- Work to develop trust with each account.
- Show up on time, every time.
- Have a real sense of urgency no matter the situation.
- Develop trust with the buyer.

Dawn's routines for success:

- Dawn begins each day with gratitude.
- She reads or listens to an audio book, 15 minutes each morning.
- She is at her desk when working at home by 8:00 AM.
- Dawn plans each day the night before.
- Dawn works from the office on Mondays, traveling the balance of the week.

What great buyers do:

- They do their homework. They show up prepared.

- They know their numbers.
- They are constantly looking for trends or changes in the marketplace.

Dawn's thoughts on the future of sales:

- Buyers love to see and touch new products. That will continue to be the case.
- There will continue to be the need for face-to-face meetings.
- Buyers will continue to want to develop relationships with salespeople and their brands.
- Dawn believes there will be less face-to-face interaction in the future.

An important tool:

- Dawn uses time-blocking. She says it's instrumental for her time management success.

Dawn's important takeaways:

- Dawn works to establish trust and to be trusted.
- Dawn realizes that to succeed, she must always be gritty and scrappy.

Pearl Utter

Pearl brings a strong service and marketing background to her work in hospitality every day. She executes because she knows her products, industry, and customers. She is a thorough planner who works to understand her customers' needs before she begins a conversation. And she understands how to manage a hectic day. Pearl manages her presentations by listening and searching for unmet needs. She continues to grow her business through knowledge of her industry, territory, and customer.

Pearl's rules for success:

- Build the discipline to always ask for the sale.
- Write everything down during a meeting.
- Have a strong follow-up program for every appointment.
- Always bring a small gift into every meeting. Never go in empty-handed.

Pearl's routine for the day ahead:

- The night before, Pearl sets up an index of things to do the next day.
- Pearl works up a list of 20 items to accomplish in the day.
- She scans e-mails for current or new information.
- She adds e-mail contacts to her database.

How Pearl overcomes a poor sales period:

- She pulls together purchases from her accounts looking for trends or opportunities.

- She uses tools to search for reasons when sales are less than expected.
- She goes over all new product detail, making certain she is ready to talk about new products, items, and programs.

Changes due to the pandemic:

- Pearl has changed her presentation based specifically on the economy of the moment.
- Pearl works to move buyers past their reluctance of what to buy, how many to purchase.
- Pearl has a new confidence. She sells and serves for the future success of her clients.
- The pandemic has made Pearl a more organized sales professional.
- Pearl works proactively on managing her time for both her work and her family.

Pearl's secret sauce:

- Her marketing background helps her succeed in sales.

Gary Baldwin

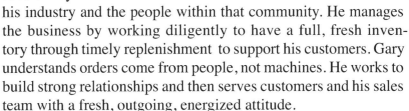

In addition to managing a national sales organization, Gary supports several key accounts. He understands his industry and the people within that community. He manages the business by working diligently to have a full, fresh inventory through timely replenishment to support his customers. Gary understands orders come from people, not machines. He works to build strong relationships and then serves customers and his sales team with a fresh, outgoing, energized attitude.

Gary's rules for success:

- Create a great first impression with a customer or prospect.
- Develop a to-do list the night before.
- Know the inventory status every day.
- Understand every customer, knowing there is no one size fits all formula.
- Develop strong communication skills.
- Know how to handle and manage rejection.

Wish I knew at 22:

- Be yourself. Be consistent every day.
- Believe in yourself, knowing that mistakes will be made.
- Try never to beat yourself up when you do not walk away with an order.

What great buyers do well:

- Great buyers are highly responsive.

- They use technology better than most.
- They are very good listeners.
- They are willing to take risks.

Gary's key habits:

- Gary always does follow-up with every customer.
- He works to convince his sales reps that they are in partnership with their accounts, helping them build a consistent revenue stream.
- Gary has a tickler file. He uses this reminder tool to reconnect with an account 60 days after an order has arrived.

Gary's important takeaways:

- Realize that everyone in sales is in the people business.
- Gary works to make his process easy for every customer.
- Do what you say you are going to do.

Sharon Holbrook

Sharon is a successful sales executive in the hospitality industry. Sharon works the "back of the house," selling the equipment and products necessary for hospitality to succeed. In her current role, Sharon not only sells key accounts, she manages a team of experienced sales professionals. Sharon loves her work and her customers. Over the years, although her corporate address has changed, her determination, hard work, and attention to detail have always made the journey. Her mantra is attention to detail.

Sharon's rules for success:

- Follow-up is critical with customers.
- Make friends with your buyers. Buyers like buying from friends.
- Treat every customer as she expects to be treated in life.

Sharon's secret sauce:

- Strives to always be authentic.
- Your first goal should be to make a friend before attempting to make a sale.

What great buyers do:

- They tell the truth.
- They do not waste her time.
- They explain the reasons for their decisions, whether positive or negative.

How Sharon sees the future of selling:

- There will be less micromanagement.
- There will be more structure within the selling process.
- Data and analytics will play a growing role in the process.
- Customer relationship management (CRM) will play a greater role for companies of all sizes.

Her keys:

- Get in front of more customers.
- A No is not permanent. Plan to see the buyer over and over, presenting other products, together with ideas to help them drive new business.
- Never be afraid of rejection.
- When you are given the opportunity to visit with a buyer over and over, you will eventually break down their resistance.

Sharon's takeaway:

- Focus on the needs of your customer.

Thom Robb

Thom is retired now but enjoyed a long, successful career. He served in more than one industry, in several different roles. Being a sales professional requires one set of skills while managing sales professionals involves a very different set of skills. Thom was intense, disciplined, and always working for his team and his customers. Thom was honest, authentic, and thorough in his approach. Because he worked with several brands, Thom had the opportunity to influence a great many sales reps and customers. He showed respect for each person he touched throughout his career.

Thom's rules for success:

- Get up early.
- Be a successful presenter; don't push products onto your customers.
- Be persistent. Make "No" your fuel.

Wish I knew at 22:

- To get out of bed every day, prepared for the day ahead.
- To be more aggressive.
- To keep moving forward.
- Never pay much attention to the word No.

What great buyers do:

- They truly listen to the sales pro.
- They know their customers.
- They have an open mind.

- They take advantage of opportunities.
- They want to know the marketing/advertising programs for the product.

What it takes to succeed:

- A conversation is required between the seller and buyer. It cannot be a one-way conversation.
- It takes communication and great teamwork with the inside team of the selling enterprise.

Thom's other success standards:

- Have a consistent and contemporary marketing plan.
- Build a strong customer service team.
- Fill customer orders on time and at 100%.
- Support the sales team when unique or emergency orders arrive.

Thom's secret sauce as a manager:

- Thom had the back of his entire sales team.
- He served the sales team — not the other way around.

Jim McHugh

Jim, now retired, was an extraordinary sales professional over several decades. While always representing top brands, Jim was the leading, most sought after sales professional in his territory. He received the first call when a brand needed a change, a top performer. He built an enduring record of success by making his customer the priority. Over his career, Jim meticulously handled issues for his customers, staying involved until solutions were found. He was professional in every presentation and thorough in his preparation. No doubt he is missed by both the brands he represented as well as the customers he served.

Jim's rules for success:

- Have integrity in all you do.
- Do what you say you are going to do.

Expectations before a sales presentation:

- Create a sales plan based on account history.
- Review previous purchases.
- Present several growth ideas.

Jim's important sales tools:

- Jim's presentation van.
- Samples.
- New technology.
- Product and local knowledge.

Daily checklist:

- Prepare samples the night before for the

specific meetings.
- Make appointments during downtime.
- Review the calendar.
- Go over each account on the schedule for that day.

What do great buyers do:
- They are prepared.
- They will outline their standards.
- They know their industry and their business.

Jim's secret sauce:
- Works to form genuine relationships.
- Works to avoid the hard sell instinct.
- Works to always be welcomed back.

Best part of the profession:
- The relationships Jim has built.
- The freedom to build his own calendar.

A key success driver:
- Great time management.

Tough part of the role:
- Making appointments. It takes patience and it takes time.

Billy Holbrook

Billy has been a top sales professional for decades, representing some of the industry's elite brands. He knows his business and the important people who truly move the needle. Today he has moved away from day-to-day sales to overseeing an entire business for an international brand. In this new role, he is showcasing a new product throughout the U.S. It's a dream job for someone who always has the pulse of the market. He'll continue to be successful because he knows no other way. He manages key accounts, an entire sales force, and the marketing side of a unique brand. He handles it with humor, class, and the willingness to do all he can for his team and his customers.

Billy's rules for success:

- Be honest.
- Work to educate your buyer.
- Lead with enthusiasm.

Thoughts about the profession after COVID:

- Billy believes more and more sales will be done beyond the face-to-face meeting.
- There is much data to work with.
- There will be more paperwork to deal with.
- In this new environment trust is essential.

Wish I knew at 22:

- To have believed in myself.
- To not have taken myself so seriously.
- To stop trying to be perfect each day with my customers.

Billy's secret sauce:

- Enthusiasm.
- The ability to read the room and ask the right questions.
- The ability to always be up and excited about the product.

The great buyers:

- They know their customers.
- They avoid buying to their personal likes.
- They execute with their customers in mind.

How he sees the future of selling:

- It will be about nurturing relationships.
- Face-to-face will be less important.
- The entire pace will move faster.
- Management will demand faster results.
- It will be more and more about digital.
- Better time management will be critical.
- Reps will have more administrative work.
- Reps will become more involved in order management.

Billy's takeaways:

- Know that there is not one way to win.
- Believe in yourself.
- Create your own style.
- Trust in yourself.

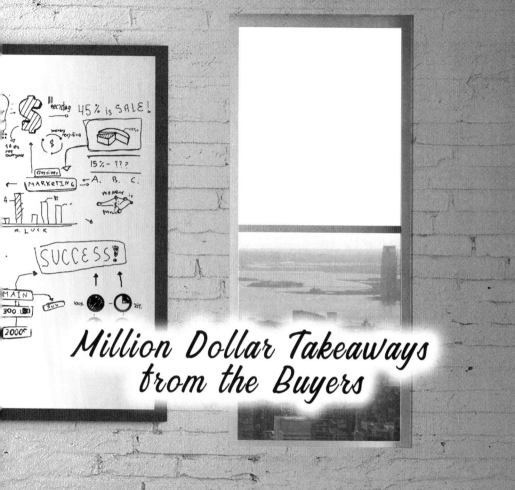

Million Dollar Takeaways from the Buyers

Kira Powell

Kira is the retail director for a large entertainment brand. Over her career, she has experienced success with several world-class organizations. As the head of retail, Kira creates programs, manages relationships, and makes purchases for all locations as well as their e-commerce site. As with other great retailers, Kira is not shy about building profit margins for her organization. She approaches her role with optimism, an expectant attitude, and the determination to drive more business for your division.

Kira's rules for success:

- Put your own opinions aside with every purchasing decision.

- Take great pain in choosing the right brands and products for the locations.

- Spend a great deal of time listening to your suppliers, team members, and customers.

- The decision to act falls on your desk each day.

- Every conversation filters through the bias and experience of people in her community.

Preparing for a supplier meeting:

- Kira looks constantly for ways to enhance the business, the presentation, and sales.

- She will change suppliers only when it will make the business better.

- Kira plans by looking for gaps in her assortment.

- Kira works hard to choose the right brands in every product class.

Wish I knew at 22:

- This is all going to work out.

Important values to possess:

- It is important to reply to a supplier and not lead people on.
- Honesty. Be upfront with the supplier.
- Take the time to listen. Do not just blow people off.

Saying No:

- Be professional.
- Be respectful.
- Things do change, so a No can turn around.
- Be totally upfront and straightforward.

Kira's secret sauce:

- She has an open mind.
- Kira works to build trust with her network of suppliers.
- Kira expects every supplier to stand behind their products.
- Potential suppliers must show a solid on-time delivery record.
- Kira will offer her customers only quality products.

Caroline Basarab

Caroline is a long-time successful buyer and merchandiser for several great organizations and a PGA Golf Professional. Through the years, she has won several regional and national awards. Caroline buys, manages inventory, builds margin, and helps execute sell-through with her teams. She is dedicated and passionate about all she does and is laser-focused on the details of buying and selling. Every location in her organization wins because Caroline serves as a partner, leader, and listener. She works hard at improving and is an industry leader respected by all.

Caroline's skills for success:

- Do your homework.
- Understand the financial side of your business.
- Create and work to maintain high standards.
- Know your industry and market.
- Be open-minded, listening to customers, suppliers, and staff.
- Work hard to be a good partner with your supplier network.
- Be forward-thinking.
- Have empathy for supplier errors.

What drives Caroline's success:

- Caroline has had several strong mentors.
- She does the necessary research.
- She works to understand the wants of her customers.
- Caroline moves around, spending little time each day at her desk.
- As a buyer, she is always observing what people are wearing.
- She engages her customers, looking for answers to enable solid future decisions.

Wish I knew at 22:

- To develop better presentation skills.
- To be more comfortable being out of the office and speaking with customers.
- Learn to be a great listener.
- Be more open-minded.
- Spend more time observing the business and customers.

Skills a buyer must have:

- Understand the retail open-to-buy programs.
- Be fanatical about being clean, neat, and fresh.
- To understand product presentation.
- To understand your market.
- To develop a strong network.
- Build a knowledgeable sales team.

Other skills to consider:

- Watch the margins daily.
- Do lots of research.
- Always keep the conversation ongoing with suppliers.
- Communicate often with your sales team.
- Demand professionalism of the team.
- Look for prompt help and support from suppliers.

Introducing new suppliers:

- Provide a premier location at the start.
- Create frequent e-blasts about the new product often, especially at the start.
- Watch sell-through closely.
- Work with the sales staff on training and energy regarding the new goods.
- Communicate the new introduction throughout the business, using the best local vehicles.

What's Next

"The best way to predict the future is to create it."
Peter Drucker.

Most books are written with some part of the past in the story. Not only providing details of past achievements, they offer to navigate through many of our present-day challenges. Although this book, filled with lessons and success takeaways, has been written to enable you to shine your light toward a greater future, it is not the grand tell-all about future discoveries, amazing shortcuts for my readers only. Although I will not provide specific predictions here, I will offer thoughts on what buying and selling might be like in the years ahead. During my career, encompassing the past six decades, speed of work has accelerated to a point where it feels ever-changing, almost out of control. In addition, the past 20 to 30 years have provided tools and other assets never before available for the world of business.

One consistent rumbling the world has heard during the past 10 years concerns extinction. The extinction of jobs: many categories of jobs. The potential list noted in various articles staggers the imagination. Where will people be working in 30 years? What might they be doing? What happens if many valuable positions disappear, replaced by AI? Certainly, these changes will spin the world a bit out of control for those who live within the bullseye. This massive potential shift will also impact education and direction for young people everywhere. How can one strategize a career if they do not know what the future menu may look like?

We can all realize one very real reality: organizations will push to do more with less. As with driverless cars, pizzas made by robots, machines pulling orders from warehouse bins, and CT scans being read by machines, companies are developing ways for artificial intelligence to do the work once done by people like you and me. To be sure, that pizza doesn't require a relationship, and neither does the warehouse robot. In sales, however, there is still the need for building relationships. The goal of a business, as

The Grand Tug of War: Buying and Selling in the Real World

quoted by management guru Peter Drucker, is to create and retain a customer. The ability to sell, service, and motivate customers to buy is still very much a human thing.

What, however, are the concerns with technology and the future need for people in the world of selling? What will the internet be able to do to support the sales process in the future? With companies like Spreetail and others, looking to disrupt the traditional paths to purchase, leaders everywhere are seeking to extract costs from any part of the sales process. What should you do? How will you mitigate the challenges already advancing in the space?

As noted above, I will not predict the future. I can, however, suggest the following:

- The internet will have a strong hand in changing the process of buying and selling.

- Organizations will continue to need great people and solid representation.

- There are many critical steps before an order is made. Relationships will continue to play a huge role in organizational growth, stability, and success.

- The higher the product price, the more valuable sales reps become.

- People will continue to be essential to customer service, especially when problems exist.

- The sales professional will become more consultant, less salesperson.

- Sales professionals will need to understand and use technology as never before.

- The sales pro will need to be all in with all phases of the customer relationship.

- Providing behind-the-curtain information will help the sales pro add the value necessary to remain distinct in a crowded world.

- The sales pro will create a closer personal relationship with accounts, as well as a closer professional relationship in working through service issues.

- The buyer will remain critical in building an initial product plan, choosing products, followed by creating a magical presentation.

- The buyer will become more of a manager and a marketer, assisting the organization well beyond the historical buying job definition.

- Although systems will predict trends, the experienced buyer will help the system see around corners, seeking out the next wave of great products and brand stories. Never underestimate an experienced feel for the business.

- The buyer will continue to work with their supplier group, developing relationships to help the organization jump to the front of the line for new product intros, detailed information, and industry issues that affect the business.

Summary

Whether you look ahead 20 or 50 years, sales professionals will be serving as buyers will be buying. It is important to note, however, that the game will continue to change and change rapidly. That means education must be top of mind for folks on both sides of the desk. People will serve, but not in the traditional ways. It's vital to adjust, become flexible, and move as the world moves. For those young professionals, aging will become an issue. When gray hair appears, the world believes you only have the knowledge and habits of days gone by. It is essential, therefore, to develop a skills program that works for both the work of today and the very different work of the future.

Almost fifty years ago I heard a prediction that sales professionals would go the way of the dinosaur, yet today, for many brands, they remain the vital connection to the customer. I believe both sales pros and buyers will continue to play important roles — just not in the traditional sense. Being flexible and open-minded will be essential for a successful future. Going above and beyond will also be an important value for the future, plus a consistent, intense follow-up strategy. As organizations hire fewer people surrounding the buyer, the salesperson can play an ever more valuable role.

There is no doubt in my mind that both buyer and seller will be doing their thing for many years to come. For those in these chairs today, be prepared to learn, unlearn, and add ever-changing assets to your skills tool kit. People will remain at the core of the exchange of goods and services. Although they may each go by the same titles, their to-do lists will not resemble those developed for your meeting next Monday morning. Being a sales professional is a great profession, a great way for people who like people to build a successful life. The buyer role for me is the greatest job in business. It is one I fell in love with decades ago and very much miss today. It was an extraordinary way for me to build a career. It was, is, and will continue to be about people. The better a person feels about the relationship, the more opportunity can be secured across the desk. With technology changing, job descriptions changing, and margins shrinking, you will need to commit to constantly adjusting your playbook to the needs of tomorrow, while at the same time, forgetting the trophies of yesterday.

One More Thing

"The secret to getting ahead is getting started."
Mark Twain

LIFE BEYOND THE TRANSACTION

This book has presented lessons, ideas, and stories on ways to improve, regardless of your side of the battle. The most successful buyers and sellers work hard. They work extra hours, extra days, and seem to always say "yes" when the call goes out for more help. They become the best because they give and keep on giving. The sacrifice is real. When you're in the office, you can't be at a ball game or dance recital. Every individual will need to decide for themselves what their commitments will be to the workplace.

This last lesson comes from personal experience. I can write about those extra days and long hours because I lived them for many years. I took every opportunity to work long hours, work days off, and more in order to drive the business and grow my career. It was not until many years later that I realized no matter what I put into a day, the work never ended. It kept coming and coming. It was my decision when to turn off the laptop and leave the unfinished work for the next day. That was an adjustment that took a bit of time.

There are a few very specific points inside this lesson.

Health: Good health is priceless! For anyone who is healthy and able to do just about anything, you are one of the richest people on the planet. We rarely appreciate the value of good health until it's been compromised or lost. Many of us are fortunate that at the start of a career, at 22 or 23, we have good health and great energy. Over time, as we age, we slow down and develop aches and ailments. We need to come up with a plan to retain or rebuild our health. After 40, good health cannot be taken for granted. I suggest you have an excellent primary care physician. The older we get, the more we must adjust to who we are at the moment. That 23-year-old is but a memory. Good health is a special gift. Do all you can to maintain it.

Downtime: Nowadays, work is 24/7, go-go-go! With smartwatches, smartphones, laptops, and tablets, we can work anytime, anywhere, which we often do. As a leader, you control your own schedule. So why not enter periods of downtime for rest and restoration? Since mental health is a real concern today, take time to get away from everything work-related, as often as you can, even for short durations. Whether it's a long weekend or several weeks, the opportunity to pursue hobbies and personal interests is a great way to relax. Be good to yourself, your family, and your organization. Schedule time to step back, do nothing, or at least change the view for a while.

Fun: Whether it's every weekend or several times a month, create some fun. Get with family or friends to do things that you all enjoy and take your mind off your to-do list. Cut that cord for a time. When life is all about work, your mind becomes cluttered and ideas stall. It becomes harder to energize your creative self. As your mind and body look forward to even small adventures, you become energized as you leave work pressures behind. Take time to explore new hobbies and interests. Building up playtime can help you better engage as you return to work.

Family: For those blessed with a family, there is nothing better. Finding a partner and experiencing children are events that cannot be matched. Most of us say we work hard for our families, but if our families were to have a say, they might vote that we be home a bit more, no matter the financial sacrifice. No matter your job or level of success, your family comes first. Do not wait on Someday Isle, that not-so-magical place, to find more time. You won't find it, and it will come when it's too late. Put your family first, because they're the reason you're working so hard. They're not there to support you while you work.

Summary

Yes, you must go the extra mile in order to reach the top. Grand success has historically not been a part of 4-day work weeks. It is about extra hours, extra days, and extra effort, but not at the sacrifice of your family, friends, and happiness. If you can create a far different plan to win, please write that book.

I just want to remind you that work is not the be-all, end-all of life. No one on their deathbed wished they had worked more. To live a full life, make good health and family your priorities. Having fun is a necessary diversion. Finding the downtime to think, travel, and do those things important to you are critical pieces to success. Although you may work hard, remember to put family first. They believe in you and trust you to do the right thing. They want quantity time and they want quality time. They deserve both.

Enjoy your career. Enjoy your life. Live on purpose every day. The clock is ticking, and it will never slow down. Make it a great life!

Acknowledgments

"A good life is a collection of happy memories."
Denis Waitley

Although we each have a community of people touching our lives in one way or another, there are others in our past. The people who helped us grow. We tend to lose sight of these folks about the time we learn to drive. We tend to forget they helped us to create our story. Writing a book is a lonely act. One sits with their computer or notepad searching for the right words in the perfect order. Staring at a blank screen most mornings is a daunting task. It begins with that first full sentence. Even if it is simply awful, the idea of laying down a new thought is a good step for the ego. In my second book, I have come to understand that whatever I write must be for me. It has to meet my standards first before I hope to gain acceptance from readers.

Writing as a quasi-perfectionist takes lots of time. Every time I reread a paragraph, I want to hit delete and start over. I often do that when I see a word that is grossly out of order. The idea of writing something that someone might want to read is humbling. In my case, I write to pass along my decades of experience and knowledge. This book came to life with the help of a few dozen experts, wonderful people who are amazing at what they do. It's an honor to include them.

I want to thank each of them for their time, generosity, and kindness. It's an amazing experience to add their special discoveries learned over decades. That has made this book so much richer.

Over the past 20 months, I have reached out over and over to these folks, to get their words just right. In providing club secrets from my years of service, along with help from my friends — who are all million-dollar producers — I believe this content can create new discoveries for years to come. To everyone in this book, I shout a grand thank you!

Over decades I have met many people. They brought light to my path, enabling me to win while I got to love what I did for work. The support begins with my wife Donna and my son JD. They are the ties that bind. Next, my siblings who put up with me from our earliest days. After that, all my friends who cared about me despite my quirky personality. Finally, the many friends in my industry that I made for parts of six decades. There is a special-ness about the golf industry that draws nice people to it. For that alone, I am beyond grateful.

In my last book, I wrote about the many hands I had the joy to shake. Here, it's the experiences I've had. Traveling around this country since the 1980s provided a wealth of connections. The people, sights, and meetings are sadly now, in my past, yet they're front and center in my bank of great memories. People, plus experiences, plus work that fit added up to a wonderful life.

Thank you,

Jack Dillon

CHECK OUT OTHER BOOKS BY JACK DILLON!

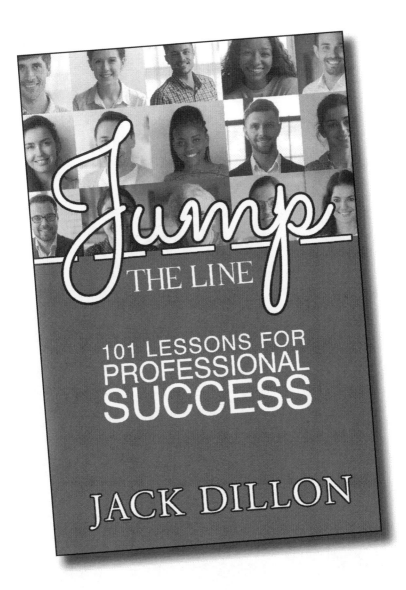

Made in the USA
Columbia, SC
01 May 2023